Layer Up!

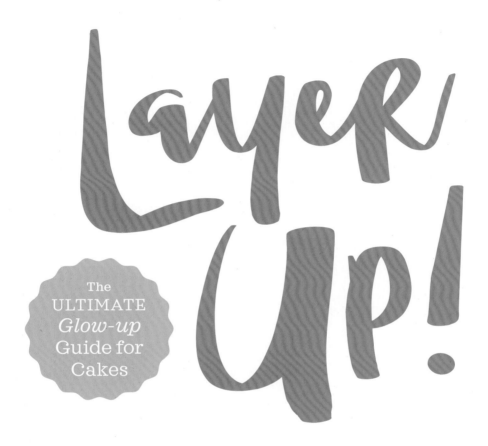

Layer Up!

The ULTIMATE *Glow-up* Guide for Cakes

YOLANDA GAMPP

PHOTOGRAPHY BY EUGENIA ZYKOVA

HTCI books

HTCI books

Published by How To Cake It Books, an imprint of Kayppin Media
(Parkland, FL).

Publishing Director: Connie Contardi

Library of Congress Control Number: 2021951462

ISBN: 978-1-938447-80-8First edition, 2022

Books may be purchased in bulk for promotional, educational, or
business use. For more information, please visit kayppin.com.

Creative Direction by Yolanda Gampp
Design by Laura Palese
Photography by Eugenia Zykova

Printed and bound in China

This book is for my mother.
The sweetest woman I've ever known,
who always loves my sweets.

• • • • • • • • • • •

I will always remember your support on my cake journey.

You told me every cake I made was beautiful.

You kept your own album of my work to show your friends.

You brewed fresh, hot coffee when I started
to fade during my long days.

You would always drive carefully while I held
onto my creations for dear life!

You would wait patiently while I finished decorating
on site and take photos.

You are simply the best mom I could ask for.

contents

How it started ...
My 1st birthday!

love letter

I ♥ cake.

My secret is out. It's been out for a while now. I fell in love with cake decorating when I was twenty-one years old, and I still love it today.

In high school, I was sure I would be an artist. My mind was a heavy rotation of daydreams in which I was a sculptor, a fashion designer, an interior designer, a painter. But the truth is, I never believed I was good enough. The pressure of producing a portfolio to present to the most prestigious art college in Toronto was a pressure I couldn't handle. I went to culinary school instead. It was the first time I felt like I knew what I was doing. The first time I truly absorbed everything around me. While I adore food (especially eating it) I discovered that my love of baking was far greater than my love of cooking.

I remember going to the dean's office and asking for his permission to apply to a bakery, rather than a restaurant, for my co-op placement. He allowed it, and, although I didn't know it that day, the decision helped set me on my path.

I started to work at the bakery on weekends, and as soon as I graduated they hired me full-time. I learned so much from the seasoned, hard-working bakers there, each one responsible for specific tasks. I have applied so much of what I learned over those years to the way I bake today. From the moment I worked the cake-decorating station I was hooked. When it comes to cake decorating, I've never looked back, only forward. I learned how to level and layer cakes properly, how to use simple syrup to prolong the life of a cake, the importance of a crumb coat and how to decorate all the cakes on their menu with different techniques.

When I reached the point where I no longer felt challenged at the bakery, I moved on to the next one. This bakery had a different approach and made a long list of desserts unlike any I had made before. Once again, I had so much to learn! But, eventually, I came to the same crossroad and I decided it was time to leave and start my own cake journey. Both bakeries did not make novelty sculpted cakes or use fondant. At the time it wasn't popular; there wasn't a single cake-decorating competition show on television. GASP! I couldn't wait to try my hand at it.

Cake has a magical way of bringing people together.

I started to make cakes in my home kitchen for everyone and anyone who would take one! Friends, family, friends of friends, neighbors. I remember feeling a constant hunger for more. Eventually I built a loyal clientele making wedding, birthday, bar mitzvah, and all kinds of special occasion cakes.

The ritual of cake decorating suits my natural tendencies. I see a vision clearly in my mind. I obsess over how I will attempt to make it. I feel determined during the transformation, and absolute joy at the result. I often had a hard time letting them go, taking as many pictures as I could long before the days where we all had cameras on our cell phones. I love creating something different every time, never repeating a cake, and having absolute freedom to create beautiful cakes. I especially love witnessing people's reactions on their special days.

Long before anyone watched me create cakes on YouTube, I was dedicated to this craft more than any other. What YouTube and How To Cake It gave me was the space to make the cakes I had only ever dreamed of, that no client had ordered—like my watermelon cake, for example. Instead of making a cake a week for one client, I made a cake a week for millions to enjoy, respond to, and try out themselves.

I must admit, writing my first book, *How To Cake It*, was one of the hardest and most rewarding experiences of my life. As soon as I was done with my first book, and before it hit the shelves, I began to daydream about this book you're holding. I am the type of person who never likes to do the same thing twice, so because my first book was dedicated to novelty cakes, I wanted this one to be dedicated to flavor profiles. I'm not even sure why, but I like to change things up and challenge myself in new ways.

Alongside my passion for novelty cakes, I also loved baking for the people I care about. Holidays, in particular, were the times I would make everything but cake. Cheesecakes, brownies, cookies, tarts, pies, and ice cream. My family and friends all have their favorites, and I've shared those recipes in this book, a collection of tried-and-true cake recipes and methods I have remained faithful to for more than twenty years.

I am so happy to share these recipes with you, and I encourage you to make them your own and share them with the people you love. Cake has a magical way of bringing people together, not only at birthdays and weddings, but even around the staff room table or the holiday office party. Everyone wants a piece!

How it's going ...

layering up

On my YouTube channel, How to Cake It, I became known for making sculpted novelty cakes that often look like everyday objects and foods that people love. I truly believe that people love to watch a transformation. I begin with layers of cake, and transform them into things everyone can recognize.

I also make what we refer to as Mega Cakes on the channel. Cakes that have a theme or a particular flavor profile, in which I layer cakes with desserts, candies, cookies, and all things sweet. I enjoyed making these cakes because they allow much more creative freedom than the weekly novelty cakes, and gave me a little break from kneading and rolling fondant, which was my only exercise for years!

Each cake is taken to the next level and stuffed with a dessert.

I find these cakes irresistible. Using flavor profiles like chocolate and peanut butter, coffee and donuts, or pink lemonade in my not-so-subtle ode to Beyoncé herself. I like to think of ways to combine cake with different fillings, textures, and nostalgic childhood favorites. In this book, I hope to teach you how to level up and layer up simple cake recipes by stuffing them full of desserts and taking them over the top. Your taste buds will thank you.

Every single cake begins with the fundamentals I believe in and subscribe to in my cake decorating career. Delicious and reliable cake recipes, kept moist and flavorful with simple syrup, a secret weapon that is standard in the bakery world but somewhat unknown to the home baker. The cakes are then filled with complementary fillings, from Italian and Swiss meringue buttercream to ganache, caramel, and frosting. These things are expected, but in order to level up and layer up, we need more.

Each cake is taken to the next level and stuffed with a dessert—whether it is a homemade recipe included in the layer up process or familiar household treats that are available at your local grocery store or donut shop.

You can make all of the components needed for these cakes in advance, and build the cake when they are all ready. Don't let the lists intimidate you, they are meant to help you organize everything you need. Take your time and enjoy the process of making each element, and then have fun layering up.

Don't have enough time to layer up? Don't worry. You can make any of the other recipes in this book as a stand-alone dessert. Whip up a batch of quick peanut butter cookies, brownies, cheesecake, or a key lime pie, the choices are endless.

Reamer

Cake tester (bamboo skewer)

Silicone pastry brush

Parchment paper

Metal cooling rack

07:21

Kitchen timer

1 2 3 4 5 6 7 8 9 10 11 12

how to cake it™

Whisk

Lil Squeeze

Measuring spoons

Candy thermometer

Ruler

Serrated Knife

Rubber spatula

tools

Silicone mat

Measuring cups

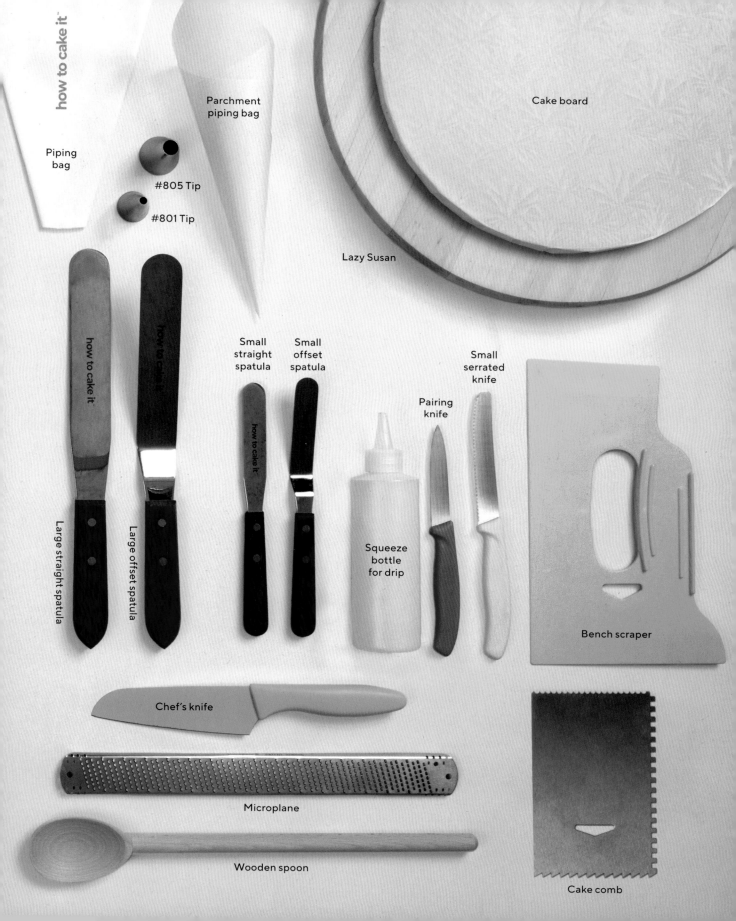

how to cake it™

Piping bag

Parchment piping bag

#805 Tip

#801 Tip

Cake board

Lazy Susan

how to cake it™

how to cake it™

how to cake it™

Small straight spatula

Small offset spatula

Small serrated knife

Pairing knife

Large straight spatula

Large offset spatula

Squeeze bottle for drip

Bench scraper

Chef's knife

Microplane

Wooden spoon

Cake comb

Dark chocolate

Dutch-processed cocoa powder

Buttermilk

ingredients

Whole milk

Butter, eggs, and dairy should always be room temperature for cake batter.

Baking powder

Baking soda

Salt

Cream of tartar

35% whipping cream

Butter

Light brown
sugar

Pure vanilla
extract

Icing sugar

Granulated sugar

Dark brown
sugar

Eggs

All-purpose
flour

1

how to
cake it

• • • • • • • • • •

HOW-TO **bake a cake**

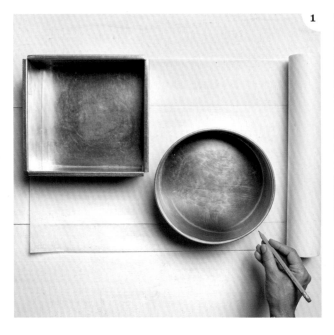

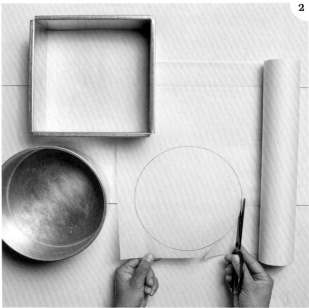

1

Preheat oven to 350°F. Place a cake pan on a sheet of parchment paper, and with a pencil, trace its outline.

2

Cut the parchment to size with scissors and use the parchment to line the bottom of the pan, spreading small bits of shortening on the bottom of the pan to secure it.

3

Scrape the batter into the prepared pan with the help of a rubber spatula—you don't want to leave any yummy batter behind!

4

If the batter is thick (like my vanilla cake batter) and doesn't naturally spread flat, smooth the top with a rubber spatula, making sure the batter reaches the edge of the pan.

5

To remove any air bubbles in the batter, run a paring knife or a straight spatula through the batter in a grid pattern, first going horizontally and then vertically. Give the pan a few good taps on your work surface to release any remaining air bubbles.

6

Set a timer for half the recommended baking time. When the timer goes off, rotate your cake pan 180 degrees. Reset the timer for 5 to 10 minutes less than the remaining baking time. Baking times are always suggestions, and all ovens are different , so it's always helpful to keep a close eye on your cakes as they bake.

7

Check the cake for doneness: Insert a cake tester or toothpick into the center of the cake and remove it. If batter or wet crumbs are stuck to the tester, continue to bake in 10-minute increments, then check again. When the cake is done, the cake tester or toothpick will come out clean.

3

5

7

9

8

Transfer the cake to a wire rack and let cool completely in the pan, then cover the pan tightly with plastic wrap and refrigerate overnight. (This helps firm up the cake so it keeps its shape.)

9

To remove the cake from the pan, loosen the edges with a straight spatula holding the flat part of the blade flush with the side of the pan and pulling along all sides. Invert the cake onto a cake board or work surface and peel off the parchment.

1

2

1

Remove the cakes from their pans and peel off the parchment. Place one cake right side up on a lazy Susan. Because the cake may not be an even height, it's important to identify the shortest side of the cake. Hold a ruler upright and flush against the shortest side of the cake and make a mark with a serrated knife just before the rounded top starts. Continue to move the ruler incrementally around the cake, marking the same measurements with the serrated knife all the way around. Place your hand on top of the cake dome and apply gentle pressure to slowly turn the lazy Susan.

2

Begin to join the marks with the serrated knife, making a shallow, continuous cut around the cake.

3

Continue to rotate the cake while you cut a little deeper, all the way around until the knife reaches the center. This is the best way to ensure a clean and even cut.

4

Lift off the dome and put it in a bowl.

5

If removing the caramelization from the bottom of your cake, turn your leveled cake upside down and remove the thin brown layer from the bottom using the same technique as you did with the leveling. I usually remove ⅛ to ¼ inch of caramelization. Add those to the scrap bowl, too.

6

To split the cake into two layers, use the ruler to find the midpoint of the side of the cake and mark it incrementally around the cake with the knife. Using the same technique that you used to level the cake, cut the cake in half.

yo's tip!

I like to use a long serrated knife so I can always see the knife on both sides of the cake. This way I can be sure I'm not digging down into the center of the cake with the tip of my knife and creating a valley.

1

Take the nozzle top off the Lil Squeeze bottle and insert the funnel. Slowly pour the simple syrup through the funnel into the bottle. Remove the funnel and replace the nozzle top. To prevent leaking, make sure you screw on the nozzle all the way, then press it down securely.

2

Hold the bottle upside down, keeping it straight, and use both hands to shower syrup onto your cake layers. Start with the outer edges and work into the center of each layer. Make sure not to oversaturate your cakes with syrup.

3

Let the syrup soak in for 5 to 10 minutes, then proceed with filling and layering. If the syrup hasn't fully soaked in, it'll make it more difficult to spread your desired filling, so make sure to give it enough time.

yo's tips!

If you don't have a Lil Squeeze bottle (they're available at howtocakeit.com), pour the simple syrup into a small bowl and brush onto the cake layers using a pastry brush. Be careful when using a natural-bristle pastry brush, as the bristles can shed onto the cake. (This is why I prefer to use Lil Squeeze.)

If the simple syrup is flavored you can choose to shower both sides of your layers for more flavor.

1

Place the first cake layer onto a cake board on a lazy Susan. Using a rubber spatula, place a big dollop of buttercream in the center of the cake layer.

2

Using a small offset spatula, start to spread the mound of buttercream over the cake layer, being careful not to scrape the surface of the cake with the spatula as it will begin to dredge up crumbs from the surface of the cake. Slowly turn the lazy Susan to help make covering the entire top easier. Spread the buttercream just a bit over the edges. If your layer of buttercream is too thin, add another small dollop and spread.

3

Use a small offset spatula to smooth the buttercream around the sides of the cake.

4

Pull the excess buttercream gathered along the top edge inward toward the center to smooth.

5

When the surface of your first cake layer is entirely covered with an even layer of buttercream, set the next cake layer on top and cover it with buttercream the same way.

6

To create a buttercream fence, fill a piping bag, fitted with an #805 round tip, with buttercream. Pipe a fence of buttercream onto the buttercream surface around the edge. Cakes with cookie crumbs, fruit, etc., between the layers will need a piped fence of buttercream to help hold the filling in. Chilling the fence before placing fillings inside adds more stability.

7

Continue to fill and stack your cake until you add the final layer.

yo's tip!

Place a non-slip mat between the lazy Susan and cake board to prevent the board from moving around as you spin.

1

Use a rubber spatula to add a dollop of buttercream to the top of your cake. Use a straight or offset spatula to move a small portion of the buttercream to the side of the cake. Spread a thin layer of buttercream all the way around the cake, pressing the crumbs into the cake as you go, and taking more buttercream from the dollop as needed. Scrape any crumb-y buttercream into the spare bowl as you go. You don't want any crumbs contaminating your gorgeous bowl of untouched buttercream.

2

When the cake sides are covered, spread the dollop of buttercream on the top of the cake. Use your spatula to go around the sides of your cake once again, smoothing any excess buttercream.

3

You'll notice a bit of excess buttercream around the top edge of the cake. Pull the buttercream into the center of the cake with your offset spatula, keeping the spatula flat on the top of your cake so that the top is covered with a thin layer and the edges are as sharp as possible. Chill for 20 to 30 minutes, until the buttercream layer is firm to the touch.

yo's tips!

This step will ensure that no crumbs will show up in your buttercream when you ice your cake.

When icing a cake after the crumb coat has chilled, the process is identical. Use the spatulas in the same way, but make sure to apply enough buttercream to the cake so that it can be smoothed, combed, or textured.

2

layer up!

· · · · · · · · · · · ·

Bountiful Breakfast

Cinnamon buns, donuts, and pancakes topped with berries and maple syrup. I'm one of those people who can never pick just one at brunch. Pour me a cup of coffee because I want it all!

CAKE №

one

cinnamon bun cake

HERE'S WHAT YOU'LL NEED TO PREP

Cake layers
Cinnamon Bun
Cake rounds 242

Syrup
Brown Sugar
Simple Syrup 249

Frosting
Cream Cheese
Frosting 272

Filling
Cinnamon Crunch
Cereal

Topping
Cinnamon Spirals
40

cinnamon Bun
cake

— **PREP IT!** —

- 3 (8-inch) Cinnamon Bun Cake rounds (page 242) 1½ recipe
- Brown Sugar Simple Syrup (page 259)
- Cream Cheese Frosting (page 272)
- 2 cups cinnamon crunch cereal
- Cinnamon Spirals (page 40)

— **LAYER UP!** —

1 Level Up & Layer Up
Remove each of the three cakes from their pans and peel off the parchment. Set the cakes right side up and level them using a ruler and serrated knife. Flip the cakes over and remove the caramelization from the bottoms using the same technique. You want all three layers to be the same height.

2 Simple Syrup
Lay the cakes out on a clean work surface, and shower them with brown sugar simple syrup. Let the syrup soak in fully before continuing.

3 First Layer
Place the first layer onto a cake board on a lazy Susan. Place a dollop of cream cheese frosting onto the center of the cake layer using the rubber spatula. Using a small offset spatula, spread the mound of cream cheese frosting over the cake layer, being careful not to scrape the surface of the cake with the spatula. Slowly turn the lazy Susan to help make covering the entire top easier.

Spread the cream cheese frosting just a bit over the edges. You want to create an even layer frosting.

4 Sprinkle It On
Sprinkle one cup of cinnamon crunch cereal onto the cream cheese frosting.

5 Pipe It On
Fill a parchment piping bag with some cream cheese frosting and cut a small hole in the tip. Starting at center of the cake, squeeze a spiral of the frosting on top of the cereal, out to the edge. This will act as glue to keep the next cake layer in place.

6 Second Layer
Place a second layer of cake on top of the first, making sure it lines up with the bottom layer. Press the layer down ever so gently. Repeat the above process; spread an even layer of cream cheese frosting, sprinkle on the remaining cereal, and pipe on a bit more frosting.

recipe continues

TOOLS

Ruler	12-inch round cake board	Small offset spatula
Serrated knife	lazy Susan	Large offset spatula
Lil Squeeze	Rubber spatula	Parchment piping bag
		Scissors

7 Third Layer
Place the final layer of cake on top, making sure it lines up.

8 Spread It
Spread another even layer of cream cheese frosting over the cake (this layer can be slightly thinner than the two layers of filling), making sure to reserve 2 tablespoons. You will use this to top your cinnamon spirals.

9 Frosting Time
Thin your 2 tablespoons of cream cheese frosting by stirring in a touch of milk or water. Place the thinned icing into a small parchment paper piping bag, or simply use a small spoon, and drizzle icing over the top of your spirals.

10 Finishing Touch
Top the cake with your beautiful cinnamon spirals.

cinnamon spirals

⅓ cup (⅔ stick) salted butter,
at room temperature,
divided

½ cup light brown sugar, packed

1 pre-rolled sheet of
frozen, all-butter puff pastry,
thawed

SPICE MIXTURE

¼ cup dark brown sugar, packed

1 teaspoon cinnamon

¼ teaspoon nutmeg

TOOLS

3 small bowls

Muffin pan

Silicone Pastry Brush

Ruler

Chef's knife

Baking sheet, lined with
parchment paper

1 Melt 1 tablespoon of butter in the microwave. Set aside.

2 In a separate bowl, stir together the remaining butter with ½ a cup light brown sugar until it forms a paste.

3 Add a ½ tablespoon of the mixture to each opening in the muffin pan, and spread to coat the bottom.

4 In a separate bowl, make the spice mixture by mixing together the ¼ cup dark brown sugar with the cinnamon and nutmeg. Set aside.

5 Unravel the sheet of puff pastry, leaving the parchment underneath. Brush the melted butter across the entire surface.

6 Sprinkle the cinnamon-spice mixture over the surface, leaving a 1-inch border along the top.

7 Roll up the pastry, starting with the bottom edge closest to you. Use the parchment paper to help you press and roll the pastry away from you. Place in the fridge for 20 minutes before cutting. While the roll is chilling, preheat the oven to 400°F.

8 Cut off the uneven ends of the pastry with a sharp knife. Cut the roll evenly into 1-inch-thick pieces. Place the pastry pieces into the muffin pan with the swirl side up.

9 Bake the cinnamon rolls for 20 to 22 minutes or until golden brown. Remove from the oven and allow to cool for 2 minutes. Carefully invert the pan onto a lined baking sheet to allow the cinnamon-spice mixture to run down the cinnamon spirals.

10 Allow the cinnamon spirals to cool completely,

CAKE N°
two

coffee & donuts cake

HERE'S WHAT YOU'LL NEED TO PREP

Cake layers

Vanilla Cake rounds
240

Chocolate Cake
round 236

Syrup

Coffee Simple
Syrup 258

Frosting

Coffee
Buttercream 262

Vanilla Buttercream
260

Fillings

Crullers

Donut holes

Instant Coffee
Concentrate

Toppings

Chocolate-dipped
donut

Sprinkled donut

coffee & donuts cake

PREP IT!

- 2 (8-inch) Vanilla Cake rounds (page 240) 1 recipe
- 1 (8-inch) Chocolate Cake round (page 236) ½ recipe
- Coffee Simple Syrup (page 258)
- 5 crullers
- 8 donut holes
- Coffee Buttercream (page 262)
- Vanilla Buttercream (page 260)
- Instant Coffee Concentrate
- 1 chocolate-dipped donut
- 1 sprinkled donut

LAYER UP!

1 Level Up & Layer Up
Remove each of the three cakes from their pans and peel off the parchment. Set the vanilla cakes right side up, and level them using a ruler and serrated knife. Flip the cakes over and remove the caramelization from the bottoms using the same technique. Now level the chocolate cake to match the height of the two vanilla layers.

2 Simple Syrup
Lay the cakes out on a clean work surface, and shower them with coffee simple syrup. Once the syrup has soaked in, flip all three layers over and shower the other side. Let the syrup soak in fully before continuing.

3 Donut Prep
Cut four of the cruller donuts and six of the chocolate donut holes in half horizontally.

4 First Layer
Place the first layer of cake onto a cake board on a lazy Susan. Place a dollop of coffee buttercream onto the surface of the cake, using the rubber spatula. Use a small offset spatula to smooth the buttercream over the surface and around the sides of the cake. Then pull the excess inward toward the center.

5 Donut Time
Arrange four cruller halves onto the buttercream with the cut side down. Make sure that the crullers remain within the perimeter of the cake. Add donut hole halves along the outer edge in the pockets of space between the crullers, and one in the center.

6 Pipe It On
Fill a piping bag fitted with an #805 round tip with coffee buttercream. Pipe buttercream into the holes of the crullers.

recipe continues

TOOLS

Ruler
Serrated knife
Lil Squeeze
Rubber spatula
Lazy Susan

12-inch round cake board
Small offset spatula
Large straight spatula
3 piping bags

3 #805 round piping tips
Bench scraper
Bamboo skewers or lollipop sticks

yo's tip!

Choose donuts that are not
heavily decorated for the inside
of your cakes. Sprinkles and
thicker glazes will dissolve inside
your cake and make a mess.

7 Second Layer
Carefully place the chocolate cake layer on top, making sure it lines up with the bottom layer. Pipe coffee buttercream into the space between the layers and smooth around the side of the cake with a small offset spatula.

8 Spread It
Repeat step 4, spreading an even layer of coffee buttercream onto the surface of the chocolate cake. Smooth the buttercream, and arrange the crullers and donut holes. Pipe coffee buttercream into the spaces.

9 Top It Off
Place the final coffee soaked vanilla cake layer on top. Remember to pipe coffee buttercream around the sides and into the space between the layers.

10 Third layer
Repeat the process, spreading an even layer of coffee buttercream onto the surface of the chocolate cake. Smooth the buttercream, arrange the crullers and donut holes, pipe coffee buttercream, then add the final coffee-soaked vanilla layer. Remember to pipe buttercream around the sides and into the space between the layers.

11 Crumb Coat & Chill
Crumb coat the whole cake in coffee buttercream and transfer to the fridge to chill.

12 Fill The Bags
Refill your piping bag with coffee buttercream. Deepen the color of the remaining coffee buttercream with more instant coffee concentrate and fill another piping bag fitted with an #805 round tip. Finally, fill a third piping bag, fitted with the same tip, with vanilla buttercream.

13 Pipe It On
Beginning at the base of the cake, pipe a ring of the deeper coffee buttercream around the perimeter. Pipe a second ring directly on top.

14 Pipe Some More
Next, pipe two concentric rings of the lighter coffee buttercream on top of the first two rings.

15 Keep On Piping
Switching to the vanilla buttercream, pipe rings all the way up to the top of the cake, and ice the top.

16 Smooth It Out
Using a small offset spatula, carefully begin to smooth the rings of buttercream. Start at the base again, moving the spatula around the cake and focus on the deeper coffee buttercream. Clean the spatula and move up to the lighter coffee buttercream, smoothing it around the cake. Clean the spatula once more and smooth the vanilla buttercream.

17 Create An Ombre
Using a bench scraper or large straight spatula, smooth the sides of the entire cake. This will create a small wall of buttercream on the top of the cake. Use the large offset spatula to pull the excess buttercream into the center and create a nice smooth and level surface.

18 Finishing Touch
Now it's time to have some fun! Arrange a selection of donuts and donut holes onto the top of the cake in any fashion you desire. You may need to use a bamboo skewer to help prop up the donuts if you wish for them to stand upright.

lemon blueberry pancake cake

HERE'S WHAT YOU'LL NEED TO PREP

Cake layers

Lemon Cake
rounds 245

Syrup

Lemon Simple
Syrup 258

Frosting

Maple Brown
Sugar Buttercream
266

Fillings

Blueberry
Preserves 56

Pancakes 54

Toppings

Mini pancakes 54

Fresh blueberries

Maple syrup.

Lemon Blueberry
pancake cake

— PREP IT! —

- 2 (8-inch) Lemon Cake rounds (page 245) 1 recipe
- Lemon Simple Syrup (page 258)
- 4 cups fresh blueberries
- Blueberry Preserves (page 56) or store-bought blueberry jam
- Maple Brown Sugar Buttercream (page 266)
- Pancakes (page 54)
- Pure maple syrup

LAYER UP!

1 Level Up & Layer Up
Remove the two cakes from their pans and peel off the parchment. Set the cakes right side up, and level them using a ruler and serrated knife. Cut each cake into two layers, for a total of four layers.

2 Simple Syrup
Lay the cakes out on a clean work surface, three of them with the cut side up and one with the caramelized surface on top. Shower the cake layers with lemon simple syrup. Let the syrup soak in fully before continuing.

3 Berry Good
Gently stir together the fresh blueberries with 2 cups of blueberry preserves to coat.

4 First Layer
Place the first layer of cake, with the caramelized surface facing down, onto a cake board on a lazy Susan. Save the second caramelized layer for the top of the cake.

5 Pipe It On
Fill a piping bag fitted with an #805 round tip with maple brown sugar buttercream. Pipe a fence of buttercream onto the cake surface around the edge. This fence will prevent your blueberry mixture from seeping out the sides of the cake.

6 Berry Delicious
Place spoonfuls of the blueberry mixture onto the cake, and spread it using a large offset spatula so that the entire layer is covered and the blueberries are nestled in the perimeter of the fence. Add more blueberries here and there, if needed, so that the whole surface is covered.

7 Pancake Time
Carefully place a large pancake on top of the first cake layer. Spread a thin layer of buttercream onto the pancake, as if you were buttering a slice of bread.

recipe continues

TOOLS

Ruler	Rubber Spatula	Small offset spatula
Serrated knife	Small bowl	Large offset spatula
Lazy Susan	Piping bag	12-inch round cake board
Simple syrup squeeze bottle	#805 round piping tip	

8 Second Layer

Place a second layer of cake on top, making sure it lines up with the bottom layer. Press the layer down ever so gently. Use a small offset spatula to smooth out the ring of buttercream between the two layers around the cake.

9 Pipe Some More

Repeat steps 5 to 8, piping a fence of maple brown sugar buttercream, followed by a layer of the blueberry mixture. Place a large pancake on top and spread a little buttercream onto its surface. Place a layer of cake on top, making sure it lines up, and smooth the buttercream around the side.

10 Top It Off

Repeat this whole process one more time, and add your final layer of cake with the caramelized side up.

11 Crumb Coat & Chill

Crumb coat the whole cake in maple brown sugar buttercream and transfer to the fridge to chill.

12 Icing On The Cake

Ice the cake and, using a small offset spatula, create horizontal ridges in the buttercream by slowly lifting the spatula up the side of the cake every time it makes one full turn on the lazy Susan. The buttercream will create a small wall, or natural fence, on top of the cake. Once you are happy with the pattern, chill the cake again.

13 Decorate It

Place a ring of mini pancakes overlapping one another on the top of the cake and spoon the remaining blueberry mixture into the center.

14 Finishing Touch

Before serving, pour pure maple syrup onto the mini pancakes.

pancakes

MAKES 3 (8-INCH) PANCAKES AND 8 MINI PANCAKES

2 cups whole fat milk

2 large eggs

¼ cup (½ stick) unsalted butter, melted

2 cups all-purpose flour

2 tablespoons granulated sugar

1 tablespoon baking powder

1 teaspoon salt

¼ cup vegetable oil

½ cup pure maple syrup

TOOLS

Whisk

Small bowl

Medium bowl

8-inch frying pan

Pancake spatula

1 cup measure

Silicone pastry brush

1 Whisk together the wet ingredients (milk, eggs, and melted butter) in a small bowl. In a medium bowl, whisk together the dry ingredients (flour, sugar, baking powder, and salt).

2 Slowly add the wet ingredients to the dry, whisking to combine.

3 Heat the frying pan on medium-high and pour a little oil onto the surface.

4 Pour 1 cup of batter into the pan. Watch the batter until multiple bubbles form on the surface. Carefully flip the pancake over and cook until you see it puff in the center, for about 1 minute. Transfer to a plate.

5 Repeat this process twice more for a total of three 8-inch round pancakes.

6 To make mini pancakes, drop the remaining batter into the pan, 1½ tablespoons at a time. You will need 6 to 8 mini pancakes for the top of the cake.

7 Once pancakes are cooked, and while they are still warm, use a silicone brush to brush the top surface of each pancake with maple syrup.

LEVEL

Up!

If you want to level up your everyday pancakes, you can make lemon blueberry pancakes by spreading **LEMON CURD (PAGE 228)** between them before you serve.

yo's tip!

Don't worry if your pancakes are not exactly 8" round. You can always trim the edges with scissors before layering them into your cake.

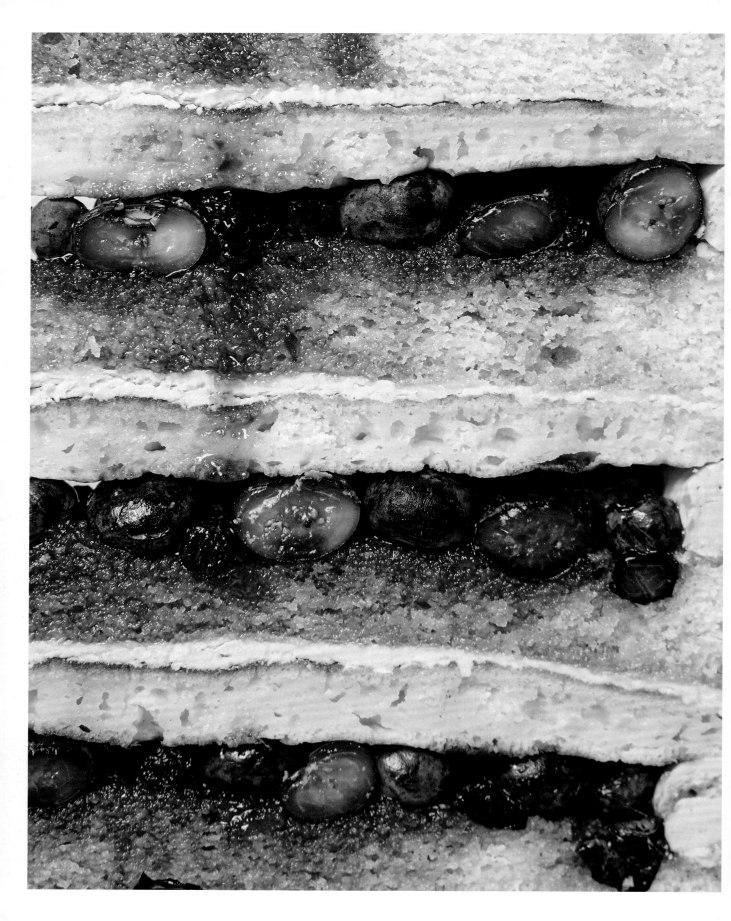

blueberry preserves

• MAKES 2½ CUPS •

3 cups granulated sugar
2 cups wild blueberries
2 tablespoons fresh lemon juice
3 tablespoons liquid pectin

TOOLS
Medium saucepan
Wooden spoon

1 Place the sugar, blueberries, and lemon juice in a medium saucepan. Bring to a boil over medium heat.

2 Stir in the liquid pectin and boil for 2 to 3 minutes.

3 Pour the preserves into a clean bowl and allow to cool completely.

cinnamon bun cake
34

Add toasted pecans to this cake if you're more of a sticky bun fan.

lemon blueberry pancake cake
48

This cake would be just as delicious with raspberries or blackberries.

coffee & donuts cake
42

Not enough coffee for you? Swap out the chocolate layer for another coffee-soaked vanilla layer.

cherished chocolate

I've always loved chocolate. It's fantastic
as a stand-alone treat, but it pairs well
with so many flavors. In my baking world -
chocolate is a girl's best friend.

chocolate coconut cake

HERE'S WHAT YOU'LL NEED TO PREP

Cake layers
Chocolate
Coconut Cake
rounds 238

Syrup
Coconut Simple
Syrup 259

Frosting
Coconut
Buttercream 263

Dark Chocolate
Ganache 270

Fillings
Chocolate-
Covered Coconut
Patties 68

Toppings
Coconut chocolate
bars

chocolate coconut
cake

— PREP IT! —

- 2 (8-inch) Chocolate Coconut Cake rounds (page 238) 1 batch
- Coconut Simple Syrup (page 259)
- Coconut Buttercream (page 263)
- Dark Chocolate Ganache (page 270) 2 recipes
- Chocolate-Covered Coconut Patties (page 68)
- 4 coconut chocolate bars (8 individual)

LAYER UP!

1 Level Up & Layer Up
Remove the two cakes from their pans and peel off the parchment. Set the cakes right side up, and level them using a ruler and serrated knife. Cut each cake into two layers, for a total of four layers.

2 Simple Syrup
Lay the cakes out on a clean work surface, and shower them with coconut simple syrup. Let the syrup soak in fully before continuing.

3 First Layer
Place the first layer of cake onto a cake board on a lazy Susan. Place a dollop of dark chocolate ganache onto the surface of the cake, using the rubber spatula. Use a small offset spatula to smooth the ganache over the surface and around the sides of the cake. Then pull the excess inward toward the center.

4 Patty Cake
Carefully place one large chocolate-covered coconut patty on top. With a large offset spatula spread an even layer of coconut buttercream.

5 Second Layer
Place a second layer of cake on top, making sure it lines up with the bottom layer. Use a small offset spatula to remove any excess buttercream between the two layers around the cake.

6 Third Layer
Spread an even layer of coconut buttercream onto the cake, then top with another layer of chocolate coconut cake.

recipe continues

TOOLS

Ruler	12-inch round cake board	Small offset spatula
Serrated knife	Lazy Susan	Large offset spatula
Lil Squeeze	Rubber spatula	Large straight spatula
		Chef's knife

yo's tip!

It helps to chill the chocolate bars in the fridge before cutting.

7 Spread It

Spread an even layer of dark chocolate ganache onto the surface, as you did with the first layer of cake. Carefully place the remaining large chocolate-covered coconut patty on top, and cover with an even layer of coconut buttercream. Use a small offset spatula to remove any excess buttercream between the two layers around the cake.

8 Top It Off

Top with the final layer of chocolate coconut cake.

9 Crumb Coat & Chill

Crumb coat the whole cake in dark chocolate ganache and transfer to the fridge to chill.

10 Icing On The Cake

Ice the cake using a large straight offset spatula. Cover the entire surface with ganache, using the spatula in a back and forth motion to create a rustic look. Once you are happy with the look, pull the excess ganache that has gathered along the top edge into toward the center of the cake, and smooth the top surface.

11 Slice It

Cut the individual coconut chocolate bars in half lengthwise **a**, as carefully as you can. Cut six of the halves, widthwise, in half **b**.

12 Finishing Touch

Place the slices of coconut chocolate bar with the coconut side out around the base of the cake, alternating between whole and half pieces. If you have trouble sticking the chocolates to the cake, spread a tiny bit of ganache on the back of each.

chocolate covered coconut patties

• MAKES 2 (8-INCH) ROUNDS •

4 cups sweetened shredded coconut

1 cup sweetened condensed milk

1 pound dark compound chocolate (melting wafers)

TOOLS

2 medium bowls

Rubber spatula

2 (8-inch) round cake pans, lined

Metal cooling rack

Baking tray

Small offset spatula

1 Pour the condensed milk over the shredded coconut in a medium bowl, and stir until combined.

2 Divide the mixture evenly between the two cake pans, and press down to compress. It helps if you wet your fingertips before pressing the mixture down.

3 Chill the patties for a minimum of 2 hours. Remove them from the pans and set them onto a metal cooling rack placed on top of a baking tray.

4 Melt the compound chocolate in the microwave in 20-second increments, making sure to stir between each. To avoid overheating the chocolate, melt it just until there are small pieces remaining. Then, stir until the pieces melt and the mixture is smooth.

5 Working with one patty at a time, pour a little chocolate onto the top and spread it out evenly using the small offset spatula. Make sure that the chocolate is not too thick. Smooth the excess chocolate around the thin sides of the patty. Repeat this process on the second patty.

6 Make sure to smooth the sides. Allow the chocolate to set completely. If desired, place the patties in the fridge to speed up the process.

7 Once the chocolate has set, carefully loosen the patties from the rack and flip them over. One at a time, pour chocolate onto the surface and spread a thin even layer. Make sure to smooth all sides. Allow to set completely.

CAKE N°
two

chocolate mint cake

HERE'S WHAT YOU'LL NEED TO PREP

Cake layers
Chocolate Cake rounds 236

Syrup
Simple Syrup 256

Frosting
Dark Chocolate Ganache 270

Mint Buttercream 262

Fillings
Mint chocolate cream cookies

Peppermint patties

Toppings
Chocolate mint thins

Chocolate mint drops

Bubbly mint chocolate bar

chocolate mint cake

— PREP IT! —

- 2 (8-inch) Chocolate Cake rounds (page 236) 1 batch
- Simple Syrup (page 256)
- Dark Chocolate Ganache (page 270)
- 32 mint chocolate cream cookies
- Mint Buttercream (page 262)
- 21 peppermint patties
- 1 box chocolate mint thins
- 1 box chocolate mint drops
- 1 bubbly mint chocolate bar

— LAYER UP! —

1 Level Up & Layer Up

Remove the two cakes from their pans and peel off the parchment. Set the cakes right side up, and level them using a ruler and serrated knife. Cut each cake into two layers, for a total of four layers.

2 Simple Syrup

Lay the cakes out on a clean work surface, and shower them with simple syrup. Let the syrup soak in fully before continuing.

3 First Layer

Place the first layer of cake onto a cake board on a lazy Susan. Place a dollop of dark chocolate ganache onto the cake using the rubber spatula. Use a small offset spatula to spread the chocolate ganache evenly over the surface and around the sides of the cake. Then pull the excess inward toward the center.

4 Line 'Em Up

Arrange a ring of mint chocolate cream cookies around the outer edge of the cake. Make sure to lay them within the perimeter of the cake so that they don't hang over the edge at all. Laying them close together you should be able to fit 11 cookies. If it is a tight squeeze, feel free to trim the final cookie to fit in the circle.

5 Second Line Up

Place a mint chocolate cream cookie in the center of the layer. Cut four cookies in half, and fan the halves around the center cookie.

6 Pipe It

Fill a piping bag fitted with an #805 tip with dark chocolate ganache. Pipe ganache into all the gaps. Pipe small mounds of ganache on top of each cookie. Carefully spread the ganache into a thin layer with a small offset spatula, trying not to disrupt the pattern.

recipe continues

TOOLS

Ruler	Lazy Susan	Piping bag
Serrated knife	Rubber spatula	2 #805 round piping tips
Lil Squeeze	Small offset spatula	Bench scraper
12-inch round cake board	Large straight spatula	Chef's knife

'yo's tip!

You can also use a bench scraper to smooth the sides of your cake.

7 Second Layer

Place a second layer of cake on top making sure it lines up with the bottom layer. Use a small offset spatula to ice away any excess ganache between the two layers around the cake.

8 Spread It

Spread an even layer of mint buttercream onto the cake. Use a small offset spatula to smooth the buttercream around the sides of the cake. Then pull the excess inward toward the center.

9 Line 'Em Up

Arrange a ring of peppermint patties around the outer edge of the cake. Make sure to lay them within the perimeter of the cake so that they don't hang over the edge at all. Laying them close together you should be able to fit 13 patties. If it is a tight squeeze, feel free to trim the final patty to fit in the circle.

10 Second Line Up

Place a peppermint patty in the center of the layer. Arrange another ring of 8 patties between the first ring and the center patty.

11 Third Layer

Place a third layer of cake on top, and as you did with the first layer, spread ganache onto the surface. Repeat the process of arranging the mint chocolate cream cookies around the outer edge and in the center of the cake, and piping and smoothing mint buttercream.

12 Top It

Top with the final layer of chocolate cake.

13 Crumb Coat & Chill

Crumb coat the whole cake in mint buttercream and transfer to the fridge to chill.

14 Icing On The Cake

Using a straight spatula, ice the entire surface of the cake with mint buttercream. Once you are happy with the look, pull the excess mint buttercream that has gathered along the top edge in toward the center of the cake, and smooth the top surface.

15 Slice It

Use a chef's knife to carefully cut the chocolate mint thins in half diagonally.

16 Decorate It

Arrange the chocolate mint thin triangles along the top edge of the cake, using the chocolate mint drops to keep each slice propped up.

17 Finishing Touch

Finely chop the bubbly mint chocolate bar. Press the crumbs around the bottom edge of the cake.

CAKE N⁰ three

chocolate peanut butter cake

HERE'S WHAT YOU'LL NEED TO PREP

Cake layers

Chocolate Cake
rounds 236

Syrup

Simple Syrup 256

Frosting

Dark Chocolate
Ganache 270

Peanut Butter
Frosting 273

Chocolate
Buttercream 268

Fillings

Peanut Butter
Blondies 82

Mini Peanut
Butter Cups

Toppings

Mini Peanut Butter Cups

Mini Quick Peanut
Butter Cookies 84

Mini salted pretzels

Roasted peanuts

Maldon Sea Salt

chocolate peanut butter cake

— PREP IT! —

- 2 (8-inch) Chocolate Cake rounds (page 236) 1 recipe
- Simple Syrup (page 256)
- Dark Chocolate Ganache (page 270)
- Peanut Butter Blondies (page 82)
- Peanut Butter Frosting (page 273)
- 22 Peanut Butter Cups
- Chocolate Buttercream (page 268)
- ½ cup Mini Peanut Butter Cups
- 8 Mini Quick Peanut Butter Cookies (page 84)
- 1 cup mini salted pretzels
- 1 cup roasted peanuts
- Maldon Sea Salt

LAYER UP!

1 Level Up & Layer Up

Remove the two cakes from their pans and peel off the parchment. Set the cakes right side up, and level them using a ruler and serrated knife. Cut each cake into two layers, for a total of four layers.

2 Simple Syrup

Lay the cakes out on a clean work surface, and shower them with simple syrup. Let the syrup soak in fully before continuing.

3 First Layer

Place the first layer of cake onto a cake board on a lazy Susan. Place a dollop of dark chocolate ganache onto the surface of the cake, using the rubber spatula. Use a small offset spatula to spread the ganache evenly over the surface of the cake.

4 Blondie

Carefully place a peanut butter blondie on top, making sure it lines up with the cake below. Use a small offset spatula to smooth the ganache around the sides of the cake.

5 Fill It

Fill one piping bag, fitted with an #805 round tip, with dark chocolate ganache. Fill the second piping bag, fitted with the same size tip, with peanut butter frosting.

6 Pipe It

Pipe a fence of ganache onto the blondie surface around the outer edge. Switch to the peanut butter frosting piping bag, and pipe a ring of frosting just inside the fence of the ganache.

7 Switch It Up

Continue to alternate piping bags, creating a bullseye pattern on the surface of the peanut butter blondie until you pipe a final dot in the center.

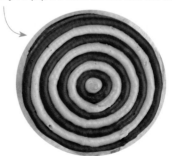

recipe continues

TOOLS

Ruler
Serrated knife
Lil Squeeze

12-inch round cake board
Lazy Susan
Rubber spatula

Small offset spatula
Large straight spatula
Piping bag
2 #805 round piping tips

8 Second Layer
Place a second layer of chocolate cake on top. Use a small offset spatula to smooth the ganache between the two layers around the cake.

9 Spread It
Spread an even layer of dark chocolate ganache onto the surface of the cake.

10 Line 'Em Up
Arrange a ring of peanut butter cups, upside down, around the outer edge of the cake. Make sure to lay them within the perimeter of the cake so that they don't hang over the edge at all. Laying them close together you should be able to fit 11 peanut butter cups. If it is a tight squeeze, feel free to trim the final peanut butter cup to fit in the circle.

11 Second Line Up
Place a second inner ring of peanut butter cups within the first formation.

12 Pipe It
Pipe peanut butter frosting into all the gaps, as well as small mounds on top of each upside down peanut butter cup. Carefully spread the frosting into a thin layer with a small offset spatula, trying not to disrupt the pattern.

13 Third Layer
Place a third layer of chocolate cake on top. Use a small offset spatula to smooth the peanut butter frosting between the two layers around the cake.

14 One More Time
Repeat step 3 one more time, spreading dark chocolate ganache onto this layer, and adding the second peanut butter blondie on top. Then pipe the same bullseye pattern of alternating ganache and frosting onto the blondie.

15 Top It Off
Add the final chocolate cake layer.

16 Crumb Coat & Chill
Crumb coat the whole cake in chocolate buttercream and transfer to the fridge to chill.

17 Ice It
Using the large straight spatula ice the sides and top of the cake with chocolate buttercream. Use the tip of a small offset spatula to draw the letter "C" in the buttercream repeatedly. Each curve does not have to be perfect or the same size. They should overlap each other as you make your way around the cake.

18 Smooth It
Once you are happy with the pattern, pull the excess buttercream that has gathered along the top edge in toward the center of the cake, and smooth the top surface.

19 Finishing Touch
Have fun decorating this cake! Use a combination of mini peanut butter cups, mini quick peanut butter cookies, mini salted pretzels, roasted peanuts, and Maldon Sea Salt to take this cake over the top. Remember, you can never have too much chocolate and peanut butter!

peanut butter blondies

• MAKES 2 (8-INCH) ROUNDS •

½ cup (1 stick) salted butter, room temperature

⅔ cup smooth peanut butter

½ cup dark brown sugar, packed

½ cup granulated sugar

1 large egg, room temperature

1 teaspoon pure vanilla extract

1 cup all-purpose flour

1 cup roasted peanuts

TOOLS

Medium saucepan

Heatproof bowl

Whisk

Rubber spatula

2 (8-inch) round cake pans, lined

1 Preheat oven to 350°F.

2 Fill the saucepan halfway with water and set it over medium heat.

3 Place the butter in the heatproof bowl and set it on top of the saucepan to melt. Once the butter has melted, add the peanut butter.

4 Remove the bowl from the heat and whisk the mixture until combined. Add both sugars and continue to whisk.

5 Add the egg and vanilla and whisk until combined.

6 Using a rubber spatula, fold in the flour, followed by the roasted peanuts.

7 Divide the batter evenly between the two prepared pans.

8 Bake for 20 minutes or until blondies are golden at the edges. Remove from the oven and allow to cool completely.

9 Carefully remove the blondies from the pans, and peel off the parchment paper.

yo's tip!

You can also bake a batch of these blondies in an 8-inch square pan and cut them into squares. Same baking temperature and time.

quick peanut butter cookies

MAKES 12-14 COOKIES, PLUS 8 MINIS

1 cup granulated sugar
1 egg
1 cup smooth peanut butter

TOOLS
Large bowl
Whisk
Cookie scoop

1 teaspoon measure
2 baking trays, lined with parchment or silicone mat
Fork

1 Preheat oven to 350°F.

2 Whisk together the sugar and egg in a large bowl.

3 Add the peanut butter and whisk until everything is combined and smooth. Chill the dough for 30 minutes.

4 Use a teaspoon to measure 8 mini balls of dough. Smooth the balls of dough by rolling them between the palms of your hands. Place them onto the prepared baking tray. Use a small scoop to portion the rest of the dough.

5 Arrange your mini balls of dough on one baking tray and your regular scoops of dough on another leaving space between them.

6 Create the classic cross hatch design by using the prongs of the fork to imprint lines in one direction, and then another. (Lightly butter the prongs of the fork if they are sticking to your dough).

7 Bake the mini cookies for 8 to 10 minutes, and bake the larger ones for 12 to 14 minutes, until slightly golden. Allow to cool completely.

yo's tip!

Make a few extra cookies in case of breakage or your need of a snack—wink wink.

chocolate coconut cake
62

For a more casual look, press shredded coconut onto the outside of this cake.

chocolate mint cake
70

You can also ice this cake in ganache if you need more chocolate with your mint.

chocolate peanut butter cake
76

Serve this cake with a side of caramel. You won't regret it.

3

dreamy desserts

I can't be the only person who dreams about desserts. Brownies, cheesecake, pineapple upside down cake, and caramel cones. Now that's what dreams are made of.

CAKE N⁰ one

caramel cone cake

HERE'S WHAT YOU'LL NEED TO PREP

Cake layers	**Syrup**	**Frosting**	**Fillings**	**Toppings**
Marble Cake rounds 246	Simple Syrup 256	Caramel Buttercream 262	Sugar cones	Chocolate Glaze 97
			Waffle cones	Waffle cone
			Salted, roasted peanuts	Sprinkles
			Caramel 274	
			Chocolate Glaze 97	

caramel cone
cake

— PREP IT! —

- 3 (8-inch) Marble Cake rounds (page 246) 1½ recipes of Vanilla and Chocolate
- Simple Syrup (page 256)
- Caramel Buttercream (page 262) 1½ recipe
- 6 sugar cones
- 6 waffle cones
- 1½ cups salted, roasted peanuts
- Caramel (page 274)
- Chocolate Glaze (page 97)
- 1 cup sprinkles

LAYER UP!

1 Level Up & Layer Up
Remove the three cakes from their pans and peel off the parchment. Set the cakes right side up, and level them using a ruler and serrated knife. Flip the cakes over and remove the caramelization from the bottoms using the same technique. Cut each cake into two layers, for a total of six layers.

2 Simple Syrup
Lay the cakes out on a clean work surface, and shower them with simple syrup. Let the syrup soak in fully before continuing.

3 First Layer
Place the first layer of cake onto a cake board on a lazy Susan. Place a dollop of caramel buttercream onto the cake using the rubber spatula. Use a small offset spatula to spread the buttercream evenly over the surface and around the sides of the cake. Then pull the excess inward toward the center.

4 Pipe It
Fill a piping bag, fitted with an #805 round tip, with caramel buttercream. Pipe a fence of buttercream onto the buttercream surface around the edge. This fence will prevent the caramel and chocolate glaze from seeping out the sides of the cake.

5 Crush It
Crush six sugar cones and four waffle cones into a bowl using your hands. Reserve two waffle cones in a safe place for your cake topper.

6 Sprinkle It
Sprinkle the buttercream surface with ¼ of the crushed cones and peanuts, making sure to keep them within the buttercream fence.

7 Fill It
Fill one squeeze bottle with caramel, and the other with chocolate glaze.

recipe continues

TOOLS

Ruler
Serrated knife
Lil Squeeze
12-inch round cake board
Lazy Susan

Rubber spatula
Small offset spatula
Large straight spatula
Piping bag
#805 piping tip

Small bowl
2 squeeze bottles
bench scraper
Circle cutters(optional)
8" lollipop stick

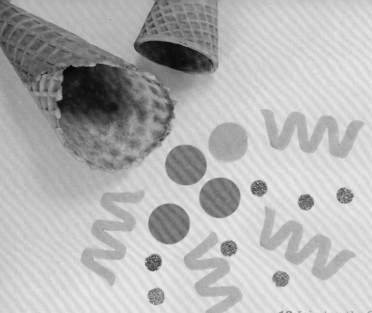

8 Drizzle It
Drizzle the chocolate glaze back and forth in one direction on top of the crushed cones and peanuts. Now, drizzle the caramel in the same manner, in the opposite direction.

9 Second Layer
Place a second layer of cake on top, making sure it lines up with the bottom layer. Press the layer down ever so gently. Use a small offset spatula to smooth out the ring of buttercream between the two layers around the cake.

10 One More Time
Repeating steps 3 to 9, build the cake up until you reach the fifth and final layer of cake. Reserve the sixth layer for the ice cream cone topper.

11 Crumb Coat & Chill
Crumb coat the whole cake in caramel buttercream and transfer to the fridge to chill.

12 Icing on the Cake
Ice the cake using a straight spatula, covering the entire surface with caramel buttercream. Use a bench scraper to smooth the sides of your cake. Once you are happy with the look, pull the excess buttercream that has gathered along the top edge in toward the center of the cake, and smooth the top surface.

13 Decorate It
Press the sprinkles gently onto the buttercream down around the bottom edge of the cake. Chill the cake for 20 minutes.

14 Top It Off
For the ice cream cone cake topper, cut circles of cake out of the sixth layer. One ¾", one 1¼", two 2", and one 2¼". Alternatively, you can crumble the cake into chunks.

15 Secure It
Carefully cut the waffle cone at the tip, removing about ½". Make sure the lollipop stick can fit through the opening.

16 Build Cone
Pipe a little caramel buttercream into the bottom of the waffle cone. Place the ¾" circle of cake inside. Pipe a little more buttercream and add the 1¼" circle. Repeat and add a 2" circle, then a 2¼" circle, and finally another 2" circle. Alternatively, fill the cone with buttercream and morsels of cake.

17 Ice It
Pipe caramel buttercream on top of the cake all around the cone. Use a small offset spatula to swirl the buttercream until you achieve the desired look.

18 Chill Out
Chill the cone for 20 mins. You can prop it up in a narrow drinking glass or wide-neck bottle

19 Mark It
Use a ruler to mark the center of the top of the cake. Push the #805 tip down into the center, about ½", and scoop out the tiny piece of cake.

20 Reheat It
Gently reheat the chocolate glaze and refill the squeeze bottle. Make sure the sauce is pourable, but not hot at all.

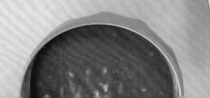

21 Create A Drip

Use the squeeze bottle to create a drip pattern along the top edge of the cake. Holding the tip of the bottle at the top edge of the cake, begin to squeeze out the chocolate sauce, allowing it to drip down the sides. Slowly move around the circumference of the cake. The more you squeeze, the longer the drips will be.

22 Space It Out

Leave space between the drips. You want to control them to achieve the nicest pattern. Think of it as a rhythm—squeeze, move, squeeze, move, etc.

23 Squeeze It

Once you have made it all the way around the cake, squeeze a good portion of the sauce onto the top of the cake.

24 Spread It

Use a small offset spatula to spread the sauce out to the edges to meet the drip border you created.

You don't want to push the glaze over the border and create more drips over the ones you carefully controlled.

25 Drip It

Use the squeeze bottle to top the ice cream cone with drip. Top the drip with a few sprinkles.

26 Top It

Insert the lollipop stick down into the center of the cake. Carefully place the decorated cone on top, making sure the exposed part of the stick enters the bottom of the cone, and press it down gently.

27 Finishing Touch

Add a few sprinkles to the top of the cake for a pop of color.

yo's tip!

Don't worry if you break you cone topper. Remember, you've got an extra one standing by.

chocolate glaze

• MAKES 2¾ CUPS •

1 pound dark chocolate, finely chopped
1 cup (2 sticks) unsalted butter
¼ cup + 1 tablespoon dark corn syrup

TOOLS

Heatproof bowl
Wooden spoon

1 Place all the ingredients in a heatproof bowl. Microwave in 30-second increments, making sure to stir between each. Do not overheat. Allow to cool, but not harden.

2 If you need to reheat the glaze, make sure to heat it gently in the microwave, in 10-second increments, stirring between each.

tropical upside down cake

HERE'S WHAT YOU'LL NEED TO PREP

Cake layers
Pineapple Coconut
Upside Down Cake 253

Syrup
Pineapple Rum Simple
Syrup 259

Frosting
Coconut Rich
Buttercream 264

Toppings
1 cup toasted coconut
chips

Pineapple Flowers 103

Maraschino cherries

tropical
upside down cake

— PREP IT! —

- 3 (8-inch) Pineapple Coconut Upside Down Cake rounds (page 253) 1 recipe
- Pineapple Rum Simple Syrup (page 259)
- Coconut Rich Buttercream (page 264)
- 1 cup toasted coconut chips
- Pineapple Flowers (page 103)
- 7 maraschino cherries

TOOLS

Ruler

Serrated knife

Toothpick

Lil Squeeze

12-inch round cake board

Lazy Susan

Rubber spatula

Small offset spatula

Large straight spatula

Fork

— LAYER UP! —

1 Level Up & Layer Up
Remove the three cakes from their pans and peel off the parchment. With the fruit side down, level them using a ruler and serrated knife.

2 Simple Syrup
Lay the cakes out on a clean work surface, and poke the surface of each cake with a toothpick several times. Shower the cakes with pineapple rum simple syrup. Let the syrup soak in fully before continuing.

3 First Layer
Place the first layer of cake, with the caramelized pineapple surface facing up, onto a cake board on a lazy Susan.

4 Spread It
Place a dollop of coconut rich buttercream onto the cake using the rubber spatula. Use a small offset spatula to spread the buttercream evenly over the surface and around the sides of the cake.

5 Second Layer
Carefully place a second layer of cake on top, fruit side up, making sure it lines up with the bottom layer. Use a small offset spatula to smooth out the ring of buttercream between the two layers around the cake.

6 Top It
Top cake with an even layer of coconut rich buttercream and add the final layer of cake, with the fruit side up.

7 Crumb Coat & Chill
Crumb coat the sidesof the cake in coconut rich buttercream and transfer to the fridge to chill.

8 Icing On The Cake
Ice the sides of the cake and smooth the buttercream with a straight spatula. The buttercream will create a small wall, or natural fence, on top of the cake. Chill the cake for 20 minutes.

9 Ice It Again
Ice another thinner layer of buttercream around the cake. Starting at the base of the cake, drag the fork prongs in an upward diagonal motion, so that they score through the buttercream.

10 Decorate It
Continue to create this pattern all the way around the cake. Now repeat this process, dragging the fork prongs in the opposite diagonal direction around the cake.

11 Finishing Touch
Decorate the base of the cake with a ring of toasted coconut chips. Create larger pineapple flowers by bunching them together, and place them on top of the cake. Add a ring of maraschino cherries to the center of the pineapple bouquet.

pineapple flowers

1 whole fresh pineapple

TOOLS
Chef's knife
Cutting board
Mandoline slicer

Muffin pan
Mini muffin pan
Baking tray, lined with
parchment paper or
Silicone mat

1 Preheat oven to 225°F.

2 Cut the top and bottom off of the pineapple. Stand the pineapple up and cut away the surrounding skin. Make diagonal cuts in a "V" shape around the pineapple to cut away the eyes.

3 Using a mandoline slicer, thinly slice the pineapple. Place the slices onto the baking tray and into the cups of the muffin pans. The tray will create flat slices and the muffin pans will create florets.

4 Bake pineapple for 1 hour, flipping the flat slices on the baking tray halfway through baking. Make the pineapple flowers a day ahead and place them in a cool dry environment to dry out further, if desired.

velvet cheesecake brownie cake

HERE'S WHAT YOU'LL NEED TO PREP

Cake layers
Red Velvet Cake rounds 254

Syrup
Simple Syrup 256

Frosting
Dark Chocolate Ganache 270

Fillings
Brownie 110

Cheesecake 108

Toppings
Cherry pie filling

velvet cheesecake
brownie cake

PREP IT!

- 2 (9-inch) Red Velvet Cake rounds (page 254) 1 batch
- Simple Syrup (page 256)
- Dark Chocolate Ganache (page 270)
- 1 Brownie (page 110)
- 1 Cheesecake (page 108)
- 1 can (20 ounces) cherry pie filling

LAYER UP!

1 Level Up & Layer Up
Remove the two red velvet cakes from their pans and peel off the parchment. Set the cakes right side up and level them using a ruler and serrated knife. Flip the cakes over and remove the caramelization from the bottoms using the same technique.

2 Trim It
Working one cake at a time, place an 8-inch round template, or bowl, on top of each cake. Use a small serrated knife to trim the caramelization away from the side of each cake, inserting the knife straight down into the cake, and cutting around the template. You want your velvet cakes to be the same diameter as your cheesecake and brownie.

3 Simple Syrup
Lay the cakes out on a clean work surface and shower them with simple syrup. Let the syrup soak in, then flip both cakes over and shower the other sides. Let the syrup soak in fully before continuing.

4 First Layer
Place the first layer of cake onto the cake board on a lazy Susan. Place a dollop of dark chocolate ganache onto the center of the cake using the rubber spatula. Using a small offset spatula, spread the mound of ganache over the cake layer, being careful not to scrape the surface of the cake with the spatula. You want to create an even layer of ganache spreading it a bit over the edges.

5 Brownie
Carefully place a brownie layer on top, and spread another layer of ganache onto it and a bit over the edges.

6 Second Layer
Place the second layer of red velvet cake on top. Use a small offset spatula to spread a third layer of ganache.

7 Cheesecake
Carefully place the cheesecake layer on top of the cake.

8 Finishing Touch
Before serving, spoon the cherry pie filling onto the top of the cheesecake.

TOOLS

Ruler	
Small serrated knife	
1 round template or bowl	

Lil Squeeze
12-inch round cake board

Lazy Susan
Rubber spatula
Small offset spatula

cheesecake

· MAKES 2 (8-INCH) ROUNDS ·

CRUST

1 cup graham cracker crumbs

¾ cup salted pretzel crumbs

⅓ cup (⅔ stick) unsalted butter, melted

¼ cup granulated sugar

BATTER

2 cups (2 bars) cream cheese, room temperature

1⅓ cups granulated sugar

1 vanilla bean

1 cup mascarpone cheese

¾ cup sour cream

½ teaspoon pure vanilla extract

3 large eggs, room temperature

½ cup all-purpose flour

TOOLS

2 (8-inch) round cake pans with removable bottoms, lined

Medium bowl

Small cake pan or glass with flat base

Stand mixer with paddle

Paring knife

Sieve

Rubber spatula

Small offset spatula

Large roasting pan

Aluminum foil

---

1 Line cake pans with parchment paper. Set aside.

2 **Make the crust:** Stir together graham cracker crumbs, salted pretzel crumbs, melted butter, and sugar in a medium bowl.

3 Divide the crumb mixture evenly between the two prepared pans. Use a smaller cake pan or a drinking glass with a flat base to press the mixture down and compress. Chill the pans in the fridge while you prepare the cheesecake batter.

4 **Make the batter:** Preheat oven to 250°F. In the bowl of a stand mixer, fitted with the paddle attachment, cream the cream cheese and sugar until smooth and fully combined.

5 In the meantime, split open the vanilla bean and scrape out the seeds with the back of a knife. Stir the seeds into the marscapone.

6 Add the mascarpone, sour cream, and vanilla extract to the cream cheese mixture. Beat on medium speed until combined.

7 Add the eggs, one at a time, and beat until combined.

8 Sift the flour directly into the batter and beat at medium speed until combined.

9 Divide the cheesecake batter evenly between the pans. Smooth the surface with a small offset spatula.

10 Wrap the bottom of each pan in a sheet of aluminum foil and place in a roasting pan large enough to fit them both.

11 Pour 1" of water into the bottom of the roasting pan. Bake cheesecakes for 1 hour and 40 minutes.

12 After the cheesecakes have cooled at room temperature, set them in the fridge for 4 hours, or overnight. I like to take it a step further by freezing them for 1 to 2 hours to allow them to set even firmer.

yo's tip!

Top this cheesecake with your favorite flavor. Chocolate ganache, caramel, or fresh berries are just a few to choose from.

brownies

· MAKES 2 (8-INCH) ROUNDS ·

12 ounces 72% dark chocolate, chopped

1 cup (2 sticks) unsalted butter

1¼ cups light brown sugar, packed

½ cup granulated sugar

½ teaspoon salt

4 large eggs, room temperature

2 large egg yolks, room temperature

1 teaspoon pure vanilla extract

1¼ cups all-purpose flour

¼ cup + 1 tablespoon Dutch-processed cocoa powder, sifted

TOOLS

2 (8-inch) round cake pans, lined

Medium saucepan

Large heatproof bowl

Rubber spatula

Whisk

1 Preheat oven to 350°F. Line cake pans with parchment paper and set aside.

2 Fill the saucepan halfway with water and set it over medium heat.

3 Place the chocolate and butter into the heatproof bowl. Place the bowl over the saucepan of simmering water, stir occasionally until melted.

4 Turn off the heat, and add the sugars and salt to the chocolate mixture. Whisk until combined.

5 Remove the bowl from the heat and add the eggs, egg yolks, and vanilla. Whisk until incorporated.

6 Fold in the flour and cocoa powder, and stir just until the dry ingredients disappear.

7 Divide batter between the prepared pans. Bake the brownies for 30 minutes, rotating the pan halfway through. Cool completely, then transfer to the fridge to chill.

yo's tip!

You can also bake this brownie batter in a 9x13 baking pan. Same temperature and baking time.

caramel cone cake
90

Instead of marble cake, try alternating layers of chocolate and vanilla.

tropical upside down cake
98

Swap the coconut batter for vanilla for a lighter version of this cake.

velvet cheesecake brownie cake
104

Not a cherry fan? Top this cake with fresh-cut strawberries before serving.

4

fan favorites

Everyone has a favorite treat that makes them feel like a kid again. Whether it's a fresh-baked chocolate chip cookie, s'mores made around a campfire, or a world-famous sandwich cookie straight out of the bag—it will bring a smile to your face.

CAKE Nº

one

chocolate chip cookie cake

HERE'S WHAT YOU'LL NEED TO PREP

Cake layers

Chocolate Chip
Cake rounds
242

Syrup

Simple Syrup
256

Frosting

Cookie Butter
Buttercream
262

Vanilla
Buttercream
260

Fillings

Chocolate Chip
Cookie layers
122

Eggless
Chocolate Chip
Cookie Dough
124

Toppings

Eggless Chocolate Chip
Cookie Dough 124

Chocolate Chip Cookies 122

Mini semi-sweet chocolate
chips

Chocolate drops

chocolate chip cookie cake

PREP IT!

- 2 (8-inch) Chocolate Chip Cake rounds (page 242) 1 recipe
- Simple Syrup (page 256)
- Cookie Butter Buttercream (page 262)
- 2 Chocolate Chip Cookie layers (page 122)
- Eggless Chocolate Chip Cookie Dough (page 124)
- Vanilla Buttercream (page 260)
- ¼ cup Semi-sweet chocolate chips
- ½ cup Mini semi-sweet chocolate chips
- Chocolate Chip Cookies (page 122)
- 6 Chocolate drops

LAYER UP!

1 Level Up & Layer Up
Remove the two cakes from their pans and peel off the parchment. Set the cakes right side up and level them with a ruler and serrated knife. Cut each cake into two layers, for a total of four layers.

2 Simple Syrup
Lay the cakes out on a clean work surface, three of them with the cut side up and one with the caramelized bottom surface on top. Shower them with simple syrup. Let the syrup soak in fully before continuing.

3 First Layer
Place the first layer of cake, with the caramelized surface facing down, onto a cake board on a lazy Susan. Save the second caramelized layer for the top of the cake.

4 Spread It
Place a dollop of cookie butter buttercream onto the cake using the rubber spatula. Use a small offset spatula to spread the cookie butter buttercream evenly over the surface of the cake.

5 Cookie
Carefully place a chocolate chip cookie layer on top, making sure it lines up with the cake below. Use a small offset spatula to smooth the cookie butter buttercream around the sides of the cake.

6 Spread It Again
Spread an even layer of cookie butter buttercream onto the surface.

7 Second Layer
Place a second layer of chocolate chip cake on top. Spread an even layer of buttercream.

8 Pipe It
Fill the piping bag, fitted with an #805 round tip, with cookie butter buttercream. Pipe a fence of buttercream onto the buttercream surface around the edge.

recipe continues

TOOLS

Ruler	Lazy Susan	Large straight spatula
Serrated knife	Rubber spatula	Piping bag
Lil Squeeze	Small offset spatula	#805 piping tip
12-inch round cake board	Small straight spatula	Bamboo skewer

9 Cookie Dough

Crumble half of the eggless cookie dough onto top of the cake so that the entire layer is covered and the morsels are nestled in the perimeter of the fence. Add more dough here and there, if you need to, so that the whole surface is covered.

10 Pipe It

Pipe dots of cookie butter buttercream onto the surface of the dough.

11 Third Layer

Place a third layer of chocolate chip cake on top. Repeat the process of the first layer by spreading cookie butter buttercream, adding a chocolate chip cookie layer, and spreading more buttercream on top.

12 Crumb Coat & Chill

Add the final layer of cake, with the caramelized side up. Crumb coat the whole cake in cookie butter buttercream and transfer to the fridge to chill.

13 Icing on the Cake

Ice the cake using a large straight spatula. Cover the entire surface, including the top, with vanilla buttercream. Smooth the sides of the cake. Once you are happy with the look, pull the excess buttercream that has gathered along the top edge inward toward the center of the cake, and smooth the top surface.

14 Create Texture

Use a small straight spatula to create vertical lines in the buttercream. Starting at the base of the cake, drag the tip of the spatula through the buttercream upward toward the top. Be careful not to press too hard or scrape the surface of the cake.

15 Decorate It

Decorate the base of the cake with crumbles of eggless cookie dough, reserving some for the top of the cake. Add chocolate chips and mini chocolate chips at the base and up along the sides, setting some aside for the top of the cake.

16 Finishing Touch

Add a crown of cookies to decorate the top of your cake using bamboo skewers carefully inserted inside each to help them stand upright. Decorate the top of the cake with the crumbles of eggless cookie dough, chocolate chips, and chocolate drops.

chocolate chip cookies & layers

• MAKES 2 (8-INCH) ROUNDS, PLUS 14 COOKIES •

2¾ cups all-purpose flour

1¼ teaspoons salt

1 teaspoon baking powder

1 teaspoon baking soda

1¼ cups unsalted butter, room temperature

1¼ cups light brown sugar, packed

¾ cup granulated sugar

1 teaspoon pure vanilla extract

2 large eggs, room temperature

1½ cups semi-sweet chocolate chips, divided

1 cup milk chocolate chips, divided

TOOLS

2 (8-inch) round cake pans, lined

Baking trays, lined with parchment paper or silicone mat

Medium bowl

Whisk

Stand mixer with paddle attachment

Kitchen scale

1 Preheat oven to 350°F.

2 Whisk together the flour, salt, baking powder, and baking soda in a medium bowl and set aside.

3 In the bowl of a stand mixer with a paddle attachment, cream together butter, both sugars, and vanilla for 3 minutes on medium speed. On the lowest speed, add the eggs one at a time and mix until fully incorporated.

4 Add the flour mixture in thirds, mixing on low speed until combined. Be careful not to overmix!

5 Pour in the semi-sweet and milk chocolate chips, reserving ¼ cup of each kind for the tops of the cookies, and mix until coated. Once the ingredients are incorporated, chill the dough for 30 minutes.

6 Use a scale to weigh out 1 pound of dough and press it into one of the prepared 8-inch round cake pans. Repeat for the second pan.

7 Portion the rest of the dough into 6 (2-ounce) portions and 8 (1.5-ounce) portions. Lightly press the portions onto the baking sheet leaving space between. You will need to bake each size cookie on a different tray.

8 Press reserved chocolate chips into the dough on the top surface of the cookies.

9 Chill the cookie layers and portioned cookies for another 30 minutes.

10 Bake the 8-inch round cookie layers for 25 to 30 minutes, the 2-ounce cookies for 10 to 12 minutes, and the 1.5-ounce cookies for 8 to 10 minutes, or until golden.

eggless chocolate chip cookie dough

• MAKES 4¼ CUPS •

2 cups all-purpose flour
1 cup salted butter, room temperature
1 cup light brown sugar, packed
½ cup granulated sugar
1 teaspoon pure vanilla extract
2 tablespoons heavy whipping cream (35%)
2 cups semi-sweet chocolate chips

TOOLS

Baking tray
Stand mixer with paddle attachment
Rubber spatula

1 Preheat oven to 350°F.

2 Spread the flour onto a baking tray. Toast in the oven for 10 to 15 minutes. Allow to cool completely.

3 In the bowl of an stand mixer fitted with the paddle attachment, cream together butter, both sugars, and vanilla at medium speed until smooth and creamy.

4 Scrape down the sides of the bowl. Add the heavy whipping cream and beat until combined.

5 With the mixer on the lowest speed, add the flour and mix until incorporated. Pour in the chocolate chips and stir to combine.

6 Chill the dough for 1 hour in the fridge.

CAKE Nº

two

cookies & cream cake

HERE'S WHAT YOU'LL NEED TO PREP

Cake layers

Black Chocolate
Cake round 238

Cookies & Cream
Cake rounds 243

Syrup

Simple Syrup 256

Frosting

Black Chocolate
Ganache 270

Chocolate
Cookie Crumb
Buttercream 262

Fillings

Double-stuffed
chocolate
sandwich cookies

Toppings

Mini chocolate
sandwich cookies

Chocolate cookie
crumbs

cookies & cream
cake

PREP IT!

- 1 (8-inch) Black Chocolate Cake round (page 238) ½ recipe
- 2 (8-inch) Cookies & Cream Cake rounds (page 243) 1 recipe
- Simple Syrup (page 256)
- Black Chocolate Ganache (page 270)
- 66 double-stuffed chocolate sandwich cookies
- Chocolate Cookie Crumb Buttercream (page 262)
- 16 mini chocolate sandwich cookies
- ¼ cup chocolate cookie crumbs

LAYER UP!

1 Level Up & Layer Up
Remove the three cakes from their pans and peel off the parchment. Set the cakes right side up and level them using a ruler and serrated knife. Cut the black chocolate cake into two layers.

2 Trim It
Place a 7-inch round cake pan upside down onto one of the chocolate cookie crumb cake rounds. Use a small serrated knife to trim the caramelization away from the side of the cake, inserting the knife straight down into the cake and cutting around the cake pan. Be extra careful not to break the chocolate cookie crumb crust at the base of the layer. Now, trim the second chocolate cookie crumb cake round and the black chocolate cake layers to the same size.

3 Simple Syrup
Lay the cakes out on a clean work surface and shower them with simple syrup. Let the syrup soak in fully before continuing.

4 First Layer
Place the first layer of cookies & cream cake, crust side down onto a cake board on a lazy Susan. Place a dollop of black chocolate ganache onto the cake using the rubber spatula. Use a small offset spatula to spread the black chocolate ganache evenly over the surface and around the sides of the cake. Then pull the excess inward toward the center.

5 Line 'Em Up
Arrange a ring of double-stuffed chocolate sandwich cookies around the outer edge of the cake. Make sure to lay them within the perimeter of the cake, so that they don't hang over the edge at all. Laying them close together, you should be able to fit 11 double-stuffed chocolate sandwich cookies. If it is a tight squeeze, feel free to trim the final cookie to fit in the circle.

recipe continues

TOOLS

Ruler	12-inch round cake board	Large straight spatula
Serrated knife	Lazy Susan	2 piping bags
7-inch round cake pan	Rubber spatula	2 #805 piping tips
Small serrated knife	Small offset spatula	Bench scraper
Lil Squeeze	Large offset spatula	Squeeze bottle

6 Second Line Up
Place a double-stuffed chocolate sandwich cookie in the center of the layer. Cut four double-stuffed chocolate sandwich cookies in half and fan the halves around the center cookie.

7 Pipe It
Fill a piping bag fitted with an #805 tip with chocolate cookie crumb buttercream. Pipe the buttercream into all the gaps and in small mounds on top of each cookie. Carefully spread the buttercream into a thin layer with a large offset spatula, trying not to disrupt the pattern below. Use a small offset spatula to ice away any excess buttercream between the two layers around the cake.

8 Second Layer
Place a layer of black chocolate cake on top. Spread an even layer of chocolate cookie crumb buttercream onto the surface. Smooth the buttercream around the sides of the cake. Then pull the excess inward toward the center.

9 Line 'Em Up
Repeat the process laying the double-stuffed chocolate sandwich cookies on top of the buttercream, creating the same formation. Pipe on more chocolate cookie crumb buttercream, and spread it into an even layer.

10 Third Layer
Place the second black chocolate cake layer on top. Spread an even layer of chocolate cookie crumb buttercream and arrange the double-stuffed chocolate sandwich cookies once again.

11 Pipe It
Fill a piping bag fitted with an #805 tip with black chocolate ganache. Pipe the ganache into all the gaps and in small mounds on top of each cookie. Carefully spread the ganache into a thin layer with a small offset spatula. You don't want to disrupt the pattern below.

12 Top it Off
Carefully place the final chocolate cookie crumb cake layer upside down on top of the ganache, with the crumb crust facing up.

13 Crumb Coat & Chill
Crumb coat the whole cake in chocolate cookie crumb buttercream. Transfer to the fridge to chill.

14 Icing On The Cake
Ice the entire surface of the cake with chocolate cookie crumb buttercream using a large straight spatula. Use a bench scraper to smooth the sides of the cake. Once you are happy with the look, pull the excess buttercream that has gathered along the top edge toward the center of the cake and smooth the top surface.

15 Reheat It
Gently reheat the remaining black chocolate ganache in 10-second intervals in the microwave, stirring between each. You want the ganache to be pourable and room temperature. Be careful not to overheat.

16 Fill It
Fill the squeeze bottle with the black chocolate ganache.

17 Create A Drip
Use the squeeze bottle to create a drip pattern along the top edge of the cake. Hold the tip of the bottle at the top edge of the cake, and begin to squeeze out the

ganache allowing it to drip down the sides. Slowly move around the circumference of the cake. The more you squeeze, the longer the drips will be.

18 Space It Out
Leave space between the drips. You want to control them to achieve the nicest pattern. Think of it like a rhythm—squeeze, move, squeeze, move, etc.

19 Squeeze It
Once you have made it all the way around the cake, squeeze a good portion of the ganache onto the top of the cake.

20 Spread It
Use a small offset spatula to spread the ganache out to the edges to meet the drip border you created. You don't want to push the ganache over the border and create more drips over the ones you carefully controlled.

21 Chill Out
Place the cake in the fridge and allow the ganache to set.

22 Decorate
Add mini chocolate sandwich cookies along the sides of the cake without interrupting the drip. Sprinkle chocolate cookie crumbs around the base.

23 Finishing Touch
Lay approximately 18 double-stuffed chocolate sandwich cookies along the top edge of the cake. Alternate the cookies so that some lay down flat and others stand up on their sides. Sprinkle a few more crumbs into the center of the cake.

s'more cake

HERE'S WHAT YOU'LL NEED TO PREP

Cake layers

Chocolate Cake
Squares 236

Graham Crusted
Chocolate Cakes
239

Syrup

Simple Syrup 256

Frosting

Dark Chocolate
Ganache 270

Toasted
Marshmallow
Buttercream 263

Fillings

Dark compound
chocolate

Toppings

Graham crackers

Milk chocolate bar

Jumbo
marshmallows

Mini marshmallows

s'more cake

- 1 (8-inch) Chocolate Cake Square (page 236) ½ recipe
- 2 (8-inch) square Graham Crusted Chocolate Cakes (page 239) 1 recipe
- Simple Syrup (page 256)
- ¼ batch Dark Chocolate Ganache (page 270)
- 1 pound dark compound chocolate (melting wafers)
- Toasted Marshmallow Buttercream (page 263)
- 8 graham crackers
- 1 (3.5-ounce) milk chocolate bar
- 4 jumbo marshmallows
- ½ cup mini marshmallows

LAYER UP!

1 Level Up & Layer Up
Remove the chocolate cake without a graham crust from its pan and peel off the parchment paper. Set the cake right side up and level it using a ruler and serrated knife. Cut the cake into two layers.

2 Simple Syrup
Flip the cakes over and lay them out on a clean work surface. Shower them with simple syrup. Let the syrup soak in fully before continuing.

3 Spread It
Place a dollop of dark chocolate ganache onto the surface of one layer using the rubber spatula. Use a small offset spatula to spread the ganache evenly over the layer. Place the second layer, simple syrup side down, on top and make sure it lines up. Use a small spatula to ice away any excess ganache from the sides.

4 Coat It
Set a metal cooking rack onto a baking tray, and place the cake onto the cooling rack. Melt the compound chocolate in the microwave in 20-second increments, making sure to stir between each. To avoid overheating the chocolate, melt it just until there are small pieces remaining, and stir until they melt and the mixture is smooth.

5 Pour It On
Pour a little chocolate onto the top surface of the cake and spread it out evenly with the small offset spatula, making sure it is not too thick. Smooth the excess chocolate around the sides of the cake.

6 Set It Up
Allow the chocolate to set completely. You can place the cake in the fridge to speed up the process.

7 One More Time
Once the chocolate has set, carefully loosen the cake from the rack and flip it over. Pour chocolate onto the surface and allow it to run down all four sides. Spread it into a thin even layer on top, and smooth the sides with a small offset spatula. Allow to set completely in the fridge.

recipe continues

TOOLS

Ruler
Serrated knife
Lil Squeeze
lazy Susan
Rubber spatula

Small offset spatula
Large offset spatula
Metal cooling rack
Baking tray
Small heatproof bowl

Spoon
Microwave-safe dish
Brûlée torch
12-inch square cake board

large offset spatula, start to spread the mound of buttercream over the cake layer, being careful not to scrape the surface of the cake with the spatula. You want to create an even layer of buttercream, spreading it just a bit over the edges.

12 Second Layer
Carefully place the chocolate-coated cake layer on top and make sure it lines up with the graham crusted cake layer.

13 Spread It
Once again, spread an even layer of toasted marshmallow buttercream onto the surface and a bit over the edges.

14 Third Layer
Place the final graham crusted chocolate cake on top with the crust side up.

15 Ice The Top
Repeat the process of spreading a layer of toasted marshmallow buttercream. Add extra swirls to the top surface with the tip of your spatula.

16 S'mores
To make a few s'mores to top the cake, lay out four graham crackers face down on a microwavable plate. Cut or break the chocolate bar into four squares.

17 Melt It
Place each square of chocolate onto a cracker. Place in the microwave for 10 seconds. If the

chocolate needs further melting, try another 10 seconds. You want the square of chocolate to become soft but not lose its shape.

18 Get Toasty
Line up the four jumbo marshmallows on the baking tray. Using the brûlée torch, carefully toast all around the sides of each marshmallow. Lift the marshmallows with a small spatula and place them onto the chocolate squares on top of the laid-out graham crackers.

19 Stack It
Place another graham cracker on top of each marshmallow and gently squeeze. If the top cracker is not sticking, spread a tiny amount of chocolate onto the bottom surface as glue. Allow the s'mores to set and stack them on top of the cake.

20 Finishing Touch
Top your cake with s'mores and a few toasted mini marshmallows.

yo's tip!

If you do not have a brûlée torch, you can thread the marshmallows through a bamboo skewer and toast them gently over an stove top burner.

8 Level Up & Layer Up
Remove the two graham crusted chocolate cakes from their pans and peel off the parchment paper. Set the cakes right side up and level them using the serrated knife.

9 Simple Syrup
Lay the cakes out on a clean work surface and shower them with simple syrup. Let the syrup soak in fully before continuing.

10 First Layer
Place the first graham crusted cake, with the crust side down onto a cake board on a lazy Susan.

11 Spread It
Place a dollop of toasted marshmallow buttercream onto the center of the layer. Using a

s'more cake

I was inspired to make this cake square because s'mores are square. It will be equally as tasty if you make it round.

chocolate chip cookie cake

Add macadamia nuts to your chocolate chip cookie layers for added crunch and buttery flavor.

cookies & cream cake

Add color to this cake by dipping your cookies in colored compound chocolate and sprinkles.

noticeably nutty

I'm a big fan of the crunch and texture that nuts can bring to a dessert. They balance the sweetness and add a rich, earthy flavor for a noticeable difference.

CAKE Nº
one

baklava cake

HERE'S WHAT YOU'LL NEED TO PREP

Cake layers

Vanilla Cake
squares 240

Syrup

Honey Simple
Syrup 259

Frosting

Honey
Buttercream 263

Fillings

Baklava squares
148

Pistachios

Liquid honey

Toppings

Baklava triangles
148

baklava cake

— PREP IT! —

- 3 (8-inch) Vanilla Cake squares (page 240) 1½ recipes
- Honey Simple Syrup (page 259)
- Honey Buttercream (page 263)
- 2 (8-inch) Baklava squares (page 148)
- 1 cup slivered pistachios
- ¼ cup liquid honey

LAYER UP!

1 Level Up & Layer Up
Remove each of the three cakes from their pans and peel off the parchment. Set the cakes right side up, and level them using a ruler and serrated knife.

2 Trim It
Using a ruler as a guide and a serrated knife, carefully cut away the caramelization from all four sides of each layer, making sure to maintain each cake's square shape.

3 Simple Syrup
Lay the cakes out on a clean work surface and shower them with honey simple syrup. Let the syrup soak in fully before continuing.

4 Spread It
Place each layer of cake onto its own cake board. Working one at a time, on a lazy Susan, place a dollop of honey buttercream onto the surface of one layer, using the rubber spatula. Use a small offset spatula to smooth the honey buttercream over the surface of the layer.

5 Crumb Coat & Chill
Crumb coat the sides of the layer. Then, pull the excess buttercream inward toward the center on top of the layer. Transfer the cake to the fridge to chill for 20 minutes.

6 One More Time
Repeat steps 4 and 5 with the two remaining layers and place them in the fridge to chill.

7 Create Texture
On one of the layers, use the tip of your small offset spatula to create texture in the buttercream. Mark the halfway point of the top of the cake. On one half of the surface, create horizontal stripes by dragging the tip of the spatula through the buttercream from one side toward the center. Be careful not to press too hard or scrape the surface of the cake.

recipe continues

TOOLS

Ruler
Serrated knife
Lil Squeeze

3 (12-inch) square cake boards
Lazy Susan

Rubber spatula
Small offset spatula
Chef's knife

8 One More Time
Use the same technique, this time to create vertical lines in the buttercream on the remaining half of the surface. Return layer to fridge to chill.

9 First Layer
Place the first chilled and iced layer of cake onto a cake board on a lazy Susan.

10 Baklava
Carefully, place a baklava layer on top, making sure it lines up with the cake below.

11 Spread It
Spread a thin layer of honey buttercream onto the surface of the baklava, mainly to act as the glue that will hold the next layer in place.

12 Decorate
Gently press ⅓ of the slivered pistachios into the buttercream at the edge of all four sides of the baklava.

13 Second Layer
Carefully, place another chilled and iced cake layer on top of the baklava, making sure it lines up with the first layer.

14 Baklava
Place the second baklava layer on top, making sure all the layers line up.

15 One More Time
Repeat steps 11 and 12, spreading more buttercream onto the surface of the baklava and pressing ⅓ of the slivered pistachios in along the sides.

16 Top It Off
Use the layer of iced cake with the textured honey buttercream as the final layer on the cake.

17 Finishing Touch
Arrange a few triangular slices of baklava along the top center of the cake, where the patterns in the buttercream meet. Drizzle the cake with honey and top with the remaining pistachio slivers.

baklava

• MAKES 2 (8x8) SQUARES & 16 TRIANGLES •

HONEY SYRUP

1 cup granulated sugar

1 cup liquid honey

BAKLAVA LAYERS

3 cups ground pistachios

3 tablespoons granulated sugar

1 package (16 sheets)
frozen phyllo pastry, thawed
in box

1 cup (2 sticks) unsalted butter,
melted

TOOLS

Medium saucepan

Medium bowl

Baking tray, lined with
parchment paper

Silicone pastry brush

Ruler

Paring knife

Chef's knife

1 Make the honey syrup: Combine the sugar and honey in the saucepan. Add 1 cup of water.

2 Bring to a boil and set aside to cool completely.

3 Make the baklava layers: Preheat oven to 375°F.

4 Mix the ground pistachios and sugar together in a bowl. Set aside.

5 Unravel the phyllo pastry. Place the trimmed parchment paper from the baking tray on top of the stack of phyllo sheets, and cut phyllo to size. Place the parchment back onto the baking tray.

6 Lay the first sheet of phyllo down on the tray. Brush the entire surface with melted butter leaving no area dry.

7 Repeat step 4 three more times, layering sheets of phyllo and butter.

8 Sprinkle one cup of the sugar and nut mixture evenly over the top sheet of buttered pastry.

9 Repeat steps 4 to 6 again, continuing to layer phyllo pastry sheets and butter on top of the nutty layer.

10 Sprinkle another cup of the sugar and nut mixture over the buttered pastry.

11 Once again, repeat step 4 to 6, continuing to layer phyllo pastry sheets and butter on top of the nutty layer.

12 Sprinkle the final cup of sugar and nut mixture over the buttered pastry.

13 Finish the baklava with the final 4 sheets of phyllo pastry, layered and brushed with butter. Place the tray in the fridge to chill for 1 hour.

14 With the chilled baklava still on the tray, use a ruler to measure and mark two 8" x 8" squares. Cut along the lines of those squares with a paring knife, making sure to cut through all the layers of pastry. Cut the remaining strip into even triangular pieces (see diagram below).

15 Bake the baklava for 25 minutes until nicely golden brown.

16 Remove from the oven and pour the honey syrup onto the hot baklava. Make sure to pour the syrup directly into the cuts in the pastry.

17 Set the baklava aside to cool and absorb all the honey syrup for at least 6 hours, or overnight.

18 If you need to, slightly trim the sides of the baklava squares with a chef's knife to clean up the edges.

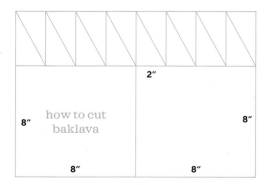

how to cut baklava

2"

8" 8"

8" 8"

CAKE Nº

two

chocolate hazelnut cake

HERE'S WHAT YOU'LL NEED TO PREP

Cake layers

Chocolate Cake
Rounds 236

Hazelnut Meringue
Rounds 156

Syrup

Simple Syrup 256

Frosting

Chocolate
Hazelnut
Buttercream 268

Fillings

Chocolate
hazelnut spread

Hazelnut creme-
filled wafers

Toppings

Hazelnut
chocolates

chocolate hazelnut
cake

— PREP IT! —

- 3 (8-inch) Chocolate Cake Rounds (page 236) 1 recipe
- Simple Syrup (page 256)
- Chocolate Hazelnut Buttercream (page 268)
- 2 (8-inch) Hazelnut Meringue Rounds (page 156)
- 1 cup chocolate hazelnut spread
- 15 hazelnut creme-filled wafers
- 4 hazelnut chocolates

— LAYER UP! —

1 Level Up & Layer Up
Remove each of the three cakes from their pans and peel off the parchment. Set the cakes right side up and level them using a ruler and serrated knife.

2 Simple Syrup
Lay the cakes out on a clean work surface and shower them with simple syrup. Let the syrup soak in fully before continuing.

3 First Layer
Place the first layer of cake onto a cake board on a lazy Susan. Place a dollop of chocolate hazelnut buttercream onto the surface using a rubber spatula. Use a small offset spatula to smooth the buttercream over the surface and around the sides of the cake. Then, with the small offset spatula, pull the excess inward toward the center.

4 Get Nutty
Carefully place a hazelnut meringue round on top, making sure it lines up with the cake below. Use a small offset spatula to smooth the chocolate hazelnut buttercream around the sides of the cake.

5 Fill It
Fill the piping bag, fitted with an #805 round tip, with chocolate hazelnut buttercream.

6 Pipe It
Pipe a fence of buttercream onto the meringue surface around the edge.

7 Spread It
Place a dollop of chocolate hazelnut spread in the center of the fence and gently spread it evenly on the surface of the meringue with a large offset spatula.

recipe continues

TOOLS

Ruler	Lazy Susan	Piping bag
Serrated knife	Rubber spatula	1 #805 piping tip
Lil Squeeze	Small offset spatula	Chefs knife
12-inch round cake board	Large offset spatula	Cutting board

8 Second Layer

Place a second layer of chocolate cake on top. Use a small offset spatula to smooth the chocolate hazelnut buttercream between the two layers around the cake.

9 Spread It

Repeat step 3. Spread an even layer of chocolate hazelnut buttercream onto the surface and smooth the edges.

10 Slice It

Use a chef's knife to cut the hazelnut creme-filled wafers diagonally in half lengthwise. Flip one half over to form a long triangle out of each rectangle.

11 Line 'Em Up

Arrange the wafers onto the buttercream so that the pointed tips are in the center of the cake and the thicker ends are at the edge to create a fan formation.

12 Pipe It

Pipe a fence of buttercream onto the surface of the wafers, around the edge.

13 Spread It

Place a dollop of chocolate hazelnut spread in the center of the fence and gently spread it evenly on the surface of the wafers with a large offset spatula.

14 Third Layer

Place a third layer of chocolate cake on top. Use a small offset spatula to smooth the chocolate hazelnut buttercream between the two layers around the cake.

15 Decorate

Repeat step 4 one more time, spreading chocolate hazelnut buttercream onto this layer and adding the second hazelnut meringue on top.

16 Finishing Touch

Top the cake with the hazelnut chocolates.

hazelnut meringues

• MAKES 2 (8-INCH) ROUNDS •

4 large egg whites, room
temperature

⅔ cup granulated sugar

8 hazelnut creme-filled wafers,
chopped

⅔ cup ground hazelnuts

⅔ cup chopped hazelnuts

¾ teaspoon baking powder

TOOLS

2 (8-inch) round cake pans,
lined along the bottom and sides

Stand mixer with whisk
attachment

Medium bowl

Rubber spatula

1 Preheat oven to 325°F.

2 In the bowl of a stand mixer fitted with the whisk attachment, whip the egg whites with the sugar until the mixture is glossy and tripled in volume, about 10 minutes.

3 Meanwhile, combine hazelnut wafers, ground hazelnuts, chopped hazelnuts, and baking powder in a bowl.

4 Remove the bowl from the mixer, and clean off the whisk attachment.

5 Fold the dry ingredients into the meringue with a rubber spatula.

6 Divide the meringue between the two prepared pans. Spread it into even layers and don't worry about making the tops perfectly smooth.

7 Bake the meringue layers for 50 minutes or until they are golden on top. Allow to cool completely.

CAKE No

three

fall harvest cake

HERE'S WHAT YOU'LL NEED TO PREP

Cake layers
Gingersnap
Crusted Carrot
Walnut Cakes
rounds 251

Syrup
Simple Syrup 256

Frosting
Maple Caramel
Buttercream 262

Fillings
Sautéed Ginger
Peaches 164

Spiced Walnuts
165

Maple Caramel
274

Toppings
Sautéed Ginger
Peaches 164

Maple Caramel
274

fall harvest
cake

— **PREP IT!** —

- 3 (8-inch) Gingersnap Crusted Carrot Walnut Cake rounds (page 251) 1 recipe
- Simple Syrup (page 256)
- Maple Caramel Buttercream (page 262)
- Sautéed Ginger Peaches (page 164)
- Spiced Walnuts (page 165)
- Maple Caramel (page 274)

LAYER UP!

1 Level Up & Layer Up
Remove each of the three cakes from their pans and peel off the parchment. Set the cakes right side up and level them using a ruler and serrated knife.

2 Simple Syrup
Lay the cakes out on a clean work surface and shower them with simple syrup. Let the syrup soak in fully before continuing.

3 First Layer
Place the first layer of gingersnap crusted carrot cake, crust side down onto a cake board on a lazy Susan. Place a dollop of maple caramel buttercream onto the cake using the rubber spatula. Use a small offset spatula to spread the buttercream evenly onto the surface and around the sides of the cake. Then pull the excess in toward the center.

4 Pipe It
Fill a piping bag fitted with an #805 round piping tip with maple caramel buttercream. Pipe a fence of buttercream onto the buttercream

surface around the edge. This fence will keep your sautéed peach slices safe inside.

5 Line 'Em Up
Arrange the sautéed peach slices by fanning them in a circle within the fence. You should be able to fit 14 to 16 slices.

6 Chop It
Chop half of the spiced walnuts, reserving the other half for the outside of the cake.

7 Sprinkle It
Sprinkle half of the chopped nuts onto the fanned peaches making sure that they remain inside the piped buttercream fence.

8 Caramel Drizzle
Fill a squeeze bottle with maple caramel. Starting on the center of the fanned peaches, squeeze a spiral of maple caramel onto the peaches continuing to spiral out until the caramel meets the fence.

recipe continues

TOOLS

Ruler
Serrated knife
Simple syrup squeeze bottle
lazy Susan

Rubber spatula
Small offset spatula
Piping bag
1 #805 round piping tip

Chef's knife
Squeeze bottle
12-inch round cake board
Cutting board

9 Second Layer

Pipe another fence directly on top of the first one, and place a second layer of cake on top making sure it lines up with the bottom layer. Press the layer down ever so gently.

10 Smooth It

Use a small offset spatula to smooth the buttercream between the layers.

11 Repeat

Repeat steps 3 to 10, spreading maple caramel buttercream, piping a fence, and filling it with sautéed peaches, half of the remaining chopped spiced nuts, and a caramel spiral.

12 Top It

Pipe a second fence and place the final layer of cake on top making sure it lines up and use an offset spatula to smooth the buttercream between the layers.

13 Crumb Coat & Chill

Spread an even layer of maple buttercream onto the top surface of the cake and lightly crumb coat the sides. Transfer the cake to the fridge to chill.

14 Finishing Touch

Arrange a fan of 12 peach slices onto the top of the cake. Top with a spiral of maple caramel, then with the reserved whole spiced nuts. Add the remaining chopped spiced nuts down along the bottom of the cake.

sautéed ginger peaches

4 large, firm peaches
½ cup (1 stick) unsalted butter
½ cup dark brown sugar, packed
4 slices fresh ginger

TOOLS

Chef's knife
Cutting board
Large frying pan

Small offset spatula
Baking tray, lined
with parchment paper or a
silicone mat
Fork

1 Quarter the peaches and slice each quarter into three slices. Set aside.

2 Place a large frying pan over medium-low heat. Melt two tablespoons of butter, and two tablespoons of brown sugar in the pan and stir until dissolved. Add the ginger and stir until fragrant.

3 Working with one peach at a time, fan 12 peach slices into the pan. Sauté until slightly softened, and use a small offset spatula to flip and coat each slice.

4 Once the peaches are tender, transfer to a baking tray and cool completely. To test the tenderness of the peach slices, pierce with a fork to make sure they are no longer hard inside. The fork should slide out easily.

5 Repeat this process until you have sautéed all of your peach slices.

yo's tip! These sautéed ginger peaches are also a nice topping for my cheesecake (see page 108)

spiced walnuts

• MAKES 1½ CUPS •

3 tablespoons unsalted butter
⅓ cup dark brown sugar
1¼ cups roasted walnuts
2 tablespoons cinnamon

TOOLS

Small saucepan
Wooden spoon
Baking tray, lined with
parchment paper or silicone mat

1 Preheat oven to 350°F.

2 Melt butter and sugar in the saucepan over medium heat.

3 Add the roasted nuts and stir until coated.

4 Add the cinnamon and stir until combined.

5 Pour nut mixture onto the prepared baking tray and bake for 10 minutes.

6 Allow to cool completely before handling.

chocolate hazelnut cake
150

Use a premium brand of chocolate hazelnut spread in this cake—you won't regret it.

baklava cake
142

Try using various types of honey for a different flavor every time. You can also swap the pistachios for hazelnuts.

fall harvest cake
158

If peaches are hard to find, try this cake with sautéed sweet plums or apples.

playful pies

When I'm not baking cakes, pies are my go-to project in any season. Apple in the cold months, key lime in the summer, and banoffee—I could eat that all year round!

CAKE N⁰ one

apple pie cake

HERE'S WHAT YOU'LL NEED TO PREP

Cake layers

Spice Cake
rounds 247

Syrup

Apple Spice
Simple Syrup
258

Frosting

Cinnamon
Brown Sugar
Buttercream
266

Fillings

Pastry discs 176

Sautéed Cinnamon
Apples 179

Pie Crumble 180

Toppings

Vanilla Buttercream
260

Lattice disc 176

Pie Crumble 180

apple pie cake

PREP IT!

- 2 (8-inch) Spice Cake rounds (page 247) 1 recipe
- Apple Spice Simple Syrup (page 258)
- Cinnamon Brown Sugar Buttercream (page 266) 1½ recipes
- Pastry discs and lattice disc (page 176)
- Sautéed Cinnamon Apples (page 179)
- Pie Crumble (page 180)
- 1 cup Vanilla Buttercream, optional (page 260)
- ½ vanilla bean, optional

LAYER UP!

1 Level Up & Layer Up
Remove both cakes from their pans and peel off the parchment. Set the cakes right side up and level them using a ruler and serrated knife. Cut each cake into two layers, for a total of four layers. If you're planning on making the ice cream scoop, make sure to reserve the cake humps!

2 Simple Syrup
Lay the cakes out on a clean work surface, three of them with the cut side up and one with the caramelized surface on top. Shower them with apple spice simple syrup. Let the syrup soak in fully before continuing.

3 First Layer
Place the first layer of cake, with the caramelized surface facing down, onto a cake board on a lazy Susan. Save the second caramelized layer for the top of the cake. Place a dollop of cinnamon

brown sugar buttercream onto the cake using the rubber spatula. Use a small offset spatula to spread the buttercream evenly over the surface and around the sides of the cake. Then pull the excess inward toward the center.

4 Pie Time
Carefully place a pastry disc onto the buttercream surface.

5 Pipe It
Fill a piping bag fitted with an #805 round tip with cinnamon brown sugar buttercream. Pipe a fence of buttercream onto the edge of the pastry surface. This fence will keep the sautéed apple slices safe inside.

6 Line 'Em Up
Arrange the sautéed apple slices by fanning them in a circle within the fence. Place the slices in the center of the circle slightly overlapping each other. You should be able to fit 20 to 24 slices.

recipe continues

TOOLS

Ruler	Lazy Susan	1 #805 piping tip
Serrated knife	Rubber spatula	2 small bowls
Lil Squeeze	Small offset spatula	Paring knife
12-inch round cake board	Large straight spatula	Cake comb
	Piping bag	

7 Pipe It
Pipe another buttercream fence on top of the first fence to build height. Pipe a couple of rings of buttercream onto the apples.

8 Second Layer
Place another layer of spice cake on top, making sure it lines up with the bottom layer, and press it down gently. Use a small offset spatula to smooth the buttercream between the two layers of cake.

9 Spread It
Repeat step 3, spreading an even layer of buttercream onto the surface of the cake layer. Then pipe a fence around the top edge.

10 Crumble
Repeat step 6, filling the fence with an arrangement of sautéed apples. Cover the apples with a layer of pie crumble.

11 Pipe It
Pipe a second fence and a couple of rings of buttercream on top of the crumble.

12 Top It Off
Place another layer of cake on top and repeat steps 3 to 7 and top with the final layer of spice cake, placing it on top with the caramelized side facing up.

13 Crumb Coat & Chill
Crumb coat the whole cake in cinnamon brown sugar buttercream and transfer to the fridge to chill.

14 Form A Scoop
Meanwhile, crumble up the cake humps into a small bowl. Mix a ½ cup of packed cake crumbs with a ¼ cup vanilla buttercream. Form this mixture into a ball, flatten the bottom, and chill.

15 Vanilla Bean
Slice open the vanilla bean using a paring knife and scrape out the seeds into a separate bowl with the back of a knife or small spatula. Stir the remaining vanilla buttercream with the vanilla seeds and set aside.

16 Icing On The Cake
Using a large straight spatula, ice the entire surface of the cake with cinnamon brown sugar buttercream. Use the cake comb to smooth the sides of the cake and create a pattern. Once you are happy with the look, pull the excess buttercream that has gathered along the top edge in toward the center of the cake, and smooth the top surface. Chill the cake once more.

17 Top The Pie
Once chilled, carefully place the baked lattice pastry on top of the cake.

18 À La Mode
Remove the cake ball from the fridge and ice it with the vanilla bean buttercream to resemble a scoop of ice cream.

19 Finishing Touch
Carefully place the scoop onto the pastry lattice. Add a few pats of vanilla bean buttercream around the bottom edge of the scoop.

yo's tip!

Save the vanilla bean pod by immersing it in a jar of sugar to create vanilla sugar. Or steep it in hot milk if you're actually making ice cream.

all butter pie dough

2¼ cups all-purpose flour,
plus extra flour for rolling

3 tablespoons granulated sugar

1 tablespoon salt

1 cup (2 sticks) unsalted butter, cold
and cut into cubes

3 tablespoons cold water

1 large egg

1 tablespoon heavy whipping cream
(35%) or milk

½ cup turbinado sugar

TOOLS

2 baking trays, lined with parchment
paper or silicone mat

Food processor

Rolling pin

7-inch round cake pan

Paring knife

Ruler

Small bowl

Whisk

Silicone pastry brush

Fork

2 (8-inch) parchment paper circles

2 (8-inch) round cake pans

Pie weights or raw beans

1 Place the flour, sugar, and salt into the food processor and process until blended.

2 Add the butter cubes a few at a time. Pulse to coat with the flour mixture before adding more.

3 Continue to pulse until the butter creates a coarse mixture. You should see crumbs of butter throughout the flour. Pour the water in slowly as you continue to pulse.

4 Pour the mixture out onto a floured surface, then lightly knead it together. Divide the dough into three and shape into discs. Wrap each disc tightly in plastic wrap. Chill for 20 minutes.

5 Roll out the dough into a circle, one disc at a time, on a floured surface until it is a ¼-inch thick. Cut out a 7½-inch circle with a sharp paring knife and place it onto one of the prepared baking trays. You can use an upside-down 7-inch cake pan, or any plate or small bowl you have in your kitchen, to help you cut a perfect circle.

6 Repeat step 5 with the second disc of dough. Place the second pie dough circle onto the tray beside the first, making sure there is space between them.

7 Roll out the third disc into a circle, and carefully cut it into ¾-inch strips. You will use these to create a lattice on the second prepared baking tray.

yo's tip!

This dough can also be
made by hand.

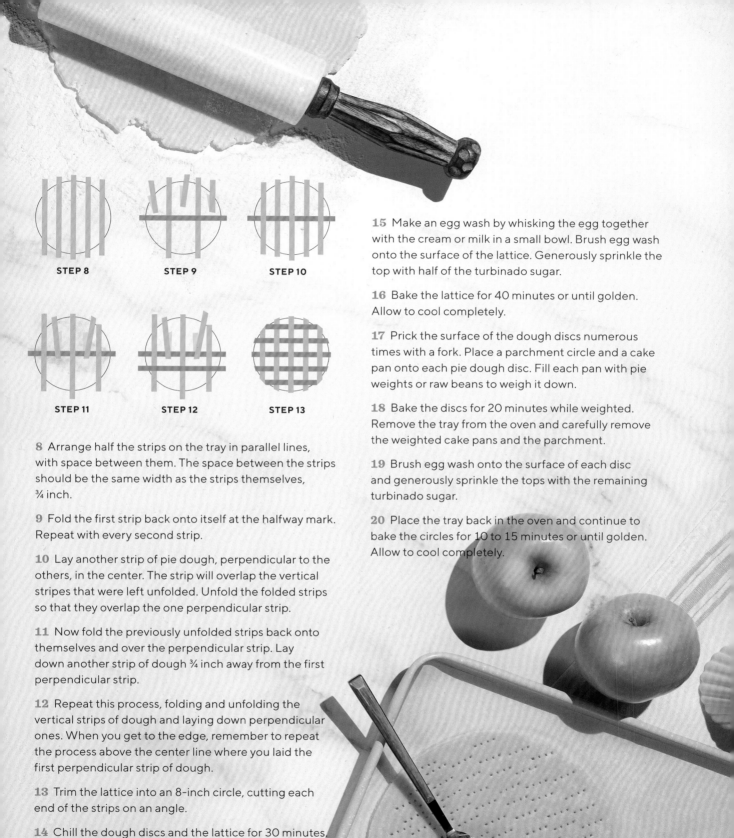

STEP 8 **STEP 9** **STEP 10**

STEP 11 **STEP 12** **STEP 13**

15 Make an egg wash by whisking the egg together with the cream or milk in a small bowl. Brush egg wash onto the surface of the lattice. Generously sprinkle the top with half of the turbinado sugar.

16 Bake the lattice for 40 minutes or until golden. Allow to cool completely.

17 Prick the surface of the dough discs numerous times with a fork. Place a parchment circle and a cake pan onto each pie dough disc. Fill each pan with pie weights or raw beans to weigh it down.

18 Bake the discs for 20 minutes while weighted. Remove the tray from the oven and carefully remove the weighted cake pans and the parchment.

19 Brush egg wash onto the surface of each disc and generously sprinkle the tops with the remaining turbinado sugar.

20 Place the tray back in the oven and continue to bake the circles for 10 to 15 minutes or until golden. Allow to cool completely.

8 Arrange half the strips on the tray in parallel lines, with space between them. The space between the strips should be the same width as the strips themselves, ¾ inch.

9 Fold the first strip back onto itself at the halfway mark. Repeat with every second strip.

10 Lay another strip of pie dough, perpendicular to the others, in the center. The strip will overlap the vertical stripes that were left unfolded. Unfold the folded strips so that they overlap the one perpendicular strip.

11 Now fold the previously unfolded strips back onto themselves and over the perpendicular strip. Lay down another strip of dough ¾ inch away from the first perpendicular strip.

12 Repeat this process, folding and unfolding the vertical strips of dough and laying down perpendicular ones. When you get to the edge, remember to repeat the process above the center line where you laid the first perpendicular strip of dough.

13 Trim the lattice into an 8-inch circle, cutting each end of the strips on an angle.

14 Chill the dough discs and the lattice for 30 minutes. Meanwhile, preheat the oven to 350°F.

sautéed cinnamon apples

4 to 6 Granny Smith apples
½ cup (1 stick) unsalted butter
½ cup dark brown sugar, packed
1 tablespoon cinnamon

TOOLS

Chef's knife
Cutting board
Large frying pan
Small offset spatula
Fork
Baking tray, lined with
parchment paper or a
silicone mat

1 Quarter the apples and core them. Then slice each quarter into four slices.

2 Melt two tablespoons of butter and two tablespoons of brown sugar in the frying pan over medium-low. Stir until dissolved. Add cinnamon.

3 Working with one apple at a time, fan 16 apple slices into the pan. Sauté until slightly softened, using a small offset spatula to flip and coat each slice. To test the tenderness of the apple slices, pierce with a fork to make sure they are no longer hard inside. The fork should slide out easily.

4 Once the apples are tender, transfer to the baking tray and let cool completely.

5 Repeat this process until you have sautéed all of the apple slices.

yo's tip!

These sautéed cinnamon apples are a lovely addition to a bowl of oatmeal or on top of ice cream. Serve out of the pan while still warm.

pie crumble

2¼ cups all-purpose
flour

1¼ cups light brown
sugar, packed

1 teaspoon cinnamon

½ teaspoon salt

1½ cups (3 sticks)
unsalted butter, cold
and cut into cubes

TOOLS

Food processor

Baking tray, lined with
parchment paper or
silicone mat

Wooden spoon

1 Preheat oven to 350°F.

2 Place flour, light brown sugar, cinnamon, and salt into
the food processor. Process until combined.

3 Add the cubes of butter and pulse to coat with the
flour mixture. Continue to pulse until the mixture
resembles coarse crumbs.

4 Pour the mixture onto the baking tray. Form clumps
by squeezing the mixture in your hands and breaking up
those clumps into large morsels.

5 Spread the crumble evenly on the tray and bake for
20 minutes, rotating and mixing with a wooden spoon
halfway through.

yo's tip!

This pie crumble can also
be made by hand. And why
not throw it on top of the
warm sautéed apples on
your ice cream.

CAKE Nº
two

banoffee
pie cake

HERE'S WHAT YOU'LL NEED TO PREP

Cake layers
Graham Crusted
Banana Cake
rounds 249

Syrup
Simple Syrup 256

Frosting
Vanilla
Buttercream 260

Fillings
Brûléed banana
slices

Caramelized
Condensed Milk
189

Toppings
White Chocolate
Whipped Cream
188

Banana Chips

banoffee pie cake

PREP IT!

- 2 (8-inch) Graham Crusted Banana Cake rounds (page 249) 1 recipe
- Simple Syrup (page 256)
- 6 to 8 bananas, ripe but firm
- ½ cup dark brown sugar, packed
- Vanilla Buttercream (page 260)
- Caramelized Condensed Milk (page 189) Or store-bought dulce de leche
- White Chocolate Whipped Cream (page 188)
- ¼ cup banana chips

LAYER UP!

1 Level Up & Layer Up
Remove both cakes from their pans and peel off the parchment. Set the cakes right side up and level them using a ruler and serrated knife. Cut each cake into two layers, for a total of four layers. You will have two layers with a crumb crust and two without.

2 Simple Syrup
Lay the cakes out on a clean work surface, and shower them with simple syrup. Let the syrup soak in fully before continuing.

3 Peel & Slice
In the meantime, peel the bananas and cut them into ½ inch slices. Line the slices up on a baking tray. Sprinkle brown sugar onto the tops of the banana slices.

4 Brûlée
Brûlée the banana slices until the brown sugar caramelizes. Allow them to cool completely.

5 First Layer
Place the first layer of graham crusted banana cake, crust side down onto the cake board on a lazy Susan. Place a dollop of vanilla buttercream onto the cake using the rubber spatula. Use a small offset spatula to smooth the buttercream around the sides of the cake. Then pull the excess inward toward the center.

6 Pipe It
Fill a piping bag, fitted with an #805 round tip, with buttercream. Pipe a fence along the edge onto the buttercream surface. This fence will hold the brûléed banana slices in place as you fill and stack.

7 Line 'Em Up
Arrange a third of the brûléed banana slices on the buttercream within the fence, making sure there are no gaps. You can trim your banana slices if needed.

recipe continues

TOOLS

Ruler	12-inch round cake board	Large straight spatula
Serrated knife	Lazy Susan	Piping bag
Lil Squeeze	Rubber spatula	1 #805 piping tip
Baking tray	Small offset spatula	Squeeze bottle
Brûlée torch		

8 Pipe It
Fill a squeeze bottle with the caramelized condensed milk. Pipe a spiral onto the banana slices, starting in the center and working your way out to the fence.

9 Second Layer
Pipe another fence directly on top of the first one, and top with a layer of crustless banana cake, making sure it lines up with the bottom layer. Press the layer down ever so gently.

10 One More Time
Repeat steps 5 to 9 and place the second layer of crustless banana cake on top.

11 And Again
Repeat steps 5 to 9 once again, and place the final layer of crusted banana cake on top with the crust side up.

12 Crumb Coat & Chill
Crumb coat the whole cake in vanilla buttercream and transfer to the fridge to chill. Use the large straight spatula and a little more buttercream to help smooth your crumb coat.

13 Finishing Touch
Top the cake with a mound of white chocolate whipped cream before serving. And add a cluster of banana chips along the base of the cake.

Note: Due to the delicate nature of bananas you'll want devour this cake quickly. The bananas will oxidize and the caramel will seep out from the cake.

yo's tip!

If you don't have a brulèe torch you can quickly place the tray of sugared banana slices under your oven broiler. But keep a close eye on them!

white chocolate whipped cream

· MAKES 1½ CUPS ·

¼ cup white chocolate, finely chopped

¾ cup + 1 tablespoon heavy whipping cream (35%)

TOOLS

Small bowl

Heatproof bowl

Rubber spatula

Stand mixer with whisk attachment

1 Place the chocolate into the small bowl. Set aside.

2 Measure 2 tablespoons of the whipping cream into a heatproof bowl and microwave in 30-second increments until it is hot.

3 Pour the hot cream over the chocolate and stir until melted.

4 Allow the ganache to cool completely. Pour the ganache and the remaining whipping cream into the bowl of a stand mixer, then stir together and chill for 30 minutes.

5 Place the chilled bowl onto the stand mixer fitted with a whisk attachment. Whip the cream on high speed until soft peaks form, about 3 minutes.

caramelized condensed milk

1 can (300 ml) sweetened
condensed milk

TOOLS
Medium saucepan
Can opener
Small bowl
Rubber spatula

1 Remove the label from the can of condensed milk. Place the can into the saucepan and cover with water.

2 Place the saucepan over medium-high heat and bring the water to a boil. Once the water boils, reduce the heat to medium and simmer for 3 hours. Make sure the can is fully submerged in water the whole time, pouring more hot water as the boiling water evaporates.

3 Remove the saucepan from the stove and cool completely. Do not attempt to remove the can from the hot water.

4 Once cool, carefully open the can and pour the condensed milk into a bowl. Stir until smooth and uniform in color. (The condensed milk tends to be deeper in color at the bottom of the can.)

CAKE No
three

key lime pie cake

HERE'S WHAT YOU'LL NEED TO PREP

Cake layers	**Syrup**	**Frosting**	**Fillings**	**Toppings**
Caramel Biscuit Crusted Lime Cake rounds 244	Lime Simple Syrup 258	Lime Buttercream 263	Lime Curd 198	Key Lime Pie 196 Green Dragées

key lime pie
cake

— PREP IT! —

- 4 (8-inch) Caramel Biscuit Crusted Lime Cake rounds (page 244) 1½ recipes
- Lime Simple Syrup (page 258)
- Lime Buttercream (page 263)
- Lime Curd (page 198)
- Key Lime Pie (page 196)
- ¼ cup of pie crumb crust (page 196) (reserved pie crumb from key lime pie recipe)
- green dragées (optional)

LAYER UP!

1 Level Up & Layer Up
Remove all four cakes from their pans and peel off the parchment. Set the cakes right side up and level them using a ruler and a serrated knife.

2 Simple Syrup
Lay the cakes out on a clean work surface and shower them with lime simple syrup. Let the syrup soak in fully before continuing.

3 First Layer
Place the first layer of caramel biscuit crusted lime cake, crust side down onto a cake board on a lazy Susan. Place a dollop of lime buttercream onto the surface of the cake, using the rubber spatula. Use a large offset spatula to smooth the lime buttercream over the surface of the layer. Ice away the excess along the sides of the cake. Then pull the excess inward toward the center.

4 Pipe It
Fill a piping bag, fitted with an #801 round tip, with lime buttercream. Pipe a fence of buttercream along the top edge onto the buttercream surface. (#801 tip pipes a smaller fence that is the perfect size to contain a thin layer of lime curd.)

5 Spread It
Place a small dollop of lime curd onto the buttercream surface. With a small offset spatula, spread it into a thin layer that remains contained within the piped fence.

6 Second Layer
Carefully place another crumb crusted lime layer of cake on top, making sure it lines up with the layer below. Use a large offset spatula to smooth the lime buttercream around the sides of the cake.

recipe continues

TOOLS

Ruler	Lazy Susan	Large straight spatula
Serrated knife	Rubber spatula	Piping bag
Lil Squeeze	Small offset spatula	1 #801 piping tip
12-inch round cake board	Large offset spatula	Silicone pastry brush

7 One More Time
Repeat steps 3 to 6, filling and stacking the cake until you place the final layer of cake on top.

8 Crumb Coat & Chill
Crumb coat the whole cake in lime buttercream and transfer to the fridge to chill.

9 Icing On The Cake
Ice the cake using a large straight spatula. Cover the entire surface with lime buttercream and ice until smooth. Once you are happy with the look, pull the excess buttercream that has gathered along the top edge in toward the center of the cake, and smooth the top surface.

10 Brush It
Use the silicone brush in a back and forth motion to create texture in the buttercream. Start by brushing along the bottom edge, all the way around the cake, and work your way up.

11 Decorate
Press the reserved ¼ cup of the key lime pie crumb crust into the buttercream around the bottom edge of the cake. Chill the cake until the buttercream is firm to the touch.

12 Finishing Touch
Carefully place the key lime pie on top of the cake. If desired, decorate the whipped cream edge of the pie with green dragées.

key lime pie

• MAKES 1 (8-INCH) ROUND PIE •

1½ cups caramel biscuit crumbs

2 tablespoons granulated sugar

⅓ cup (⅔ stick) unsalted butter, melted

1 can (300 ml) sweetened condensed milk

⅓ cup fresh lime juice (3-4 limes)

2 large egg yolks

2 tablespoons lime zest (from about 4 limes)

1 teaspoon unflavored gelatin

¾ cup heavy whipping cream (35%)

¼ cup icing sugar

TOOLS

8-inch round fluted tart pan with removable bottom

Small bowl

Rubber spatula

Small cake pan or glass with flat base

Baking tray

Medium bowl

Whisk

Small offset spatula

Stand mixer with whisk attachment

Microwave-safe bowl

Piping bag

1 #863 French star piping tip

1 Preheat oven to 350°F.

2 **Make the crust:** Mix the crumbs and sugar together in a small bowl. Add the melted butter and combine until all the crumbs are coated.

3 Set aside ¼ cup of the cookie crumb mixture. (You will use this to decorate your Key Lime Pie Cake.)

4 Press the remaining mixture along the sides and bottom of the fluted pie pan. Make sure the sides are even. Use a small cake pan or a drinking glass with a flat base to press the mixture down and compress.

5 Place the tart pan onto the baking tray and bake the crumb crust for 10 minutes. Allow to cool.

6 **Make the filling:** In the meantime, whisk together sweetened condensed milk, lime juice, egg yolks, and lime zest in a medium bowl. Once the crust is cool, pour the filling into the crust and smooth the surface with a small offset spatula.

7 Return the tart to the oven and bake for 25 minutes. Remove from the oven and allow to cool completely at room temperature. Then transfer the tart to the fridge to chill overnight.

8 **Make the whipped cream:** Place the whipping cream in the bowl of a stand mixer and transfer to the fridge to chill for 20 minutes.

9 Meanwhile, place 1½ tablespoons of water into the microwave-safe bowl. Sprinkle the gelatin on top and let sit for 5 minutes. Heat the mixture in the microwave for 10 seconds or until dissolved.

10 Remove the stand mixer bowl from the fridge and add the icing sugar. Place the bowl onto the stand mixer fitted with a whisk attachment. Whip on high speed until soft peaks form.

11 Turn the mixer to low speed and slowly add the liquid gelatin. Turn the mixer back up to high and whip the cream until stiff peaks form.

12 Fill the piping bag fitted with an #863 tip with the stabilized whipped cream.

13 Pipe little puffs along the edge of the key lime pie in various sizes, to create a border.

LEVEL Up!

Use a microplane to zest your limes, or any citrus fruit as its much more effective than a grater.

lime curd

· MAKES 1½ CUPS ·

½ tablespoon lime zest (1 lime)
½ cup granulated sugar
5 large egg yolks

1 large egg
⅓ cup fresh lime juice (3-4 limes)
2 tablespoons (¼ stick)
unsalted butter

TOOLS
Small saucepan
Large stainless steel bowl
Whisk
Wooden spoon
Medium bowl

1 Fill the saucepan half-way with water and place on the stove until simmering.

2 Whisk together lime zest and sugar in a large stainless steel bowl. Add egg yolks and eggs and whisk to combine. Finally, whisk in the lime juice.

3 Place the bowl onto the saucepan over the simmering water. Let the curd thicken over medium heat, whisking from time to time. Cook for 20 to 25 minutes or until the curd is thick.

4 Remove the bowl from the heat and add the butter. Let the butter melt and then stir it into the lime curd with a wooden spoon.

5 Transfer the curd to a medium bowl. Press plastic wrap directly on top of curd. Allow curd to cool completely, and place in the fridge.

yo's tip!

You only need one batch of lime curd to flavor the lime buttercream. The remaining will fill the cake.

banoffee pie cake
182

Level up and drizzle chocolate ganache over the brûléed bananas for extra decadence.

key lime pie cake
190

Try this cake with a different crust. Graham or chocolate cookie crumbs will both work well.

apple pie cake
170

A peach pie version of this cake would be delicious. Sauté peaches instead of apples if they are in season.

CHAPTER · 7 ·

wonderfully whimsical

If you can't have fun with cake, when can you have fun?! I'll be the first to admit that cake decorating comes with restrictions—but I never let that restrict my imagination!

CAKE № **one**

cakefetti cake

HERE'S WHAT YOU'LL NEED TO PREP

Cake layers

Cakefetti Cake
squares 245

Syrup

Simple Syrup 256

Frosting

Vanilla
Buttercream 260

Fillings

Crispy Cakefetti
Squares 210

Toppings

Crispy Cakefetti
Squares 210

Marshmallows

Rainbow sprinkles

cakefetti cake

— PREP IT! —

- 3 (8-inch) Cakefetti Cake squares (page 245) 1½ recipes
- Simple Syrup (page 256)
- Vanilla Buttercream (page 260) 2 recipes
- 2 Crispy Cakefetti Squares (page 210)
- 1 Crispy Cakefetti Square, thick
- gel food coloring in pink, purple and orange
- 12 marshmallows
- 2 tablespoons clear piping gel
- pink and purple sanding sugar
- ¼ cup rainbow sprinkles

LAYER UP!

1 Level Up & Layer Up
Remove the three cakes from their pans and peel off the parchment. Set the cakes right side up, and level them using a ruler and serrated knife. Flip the cakes over and remove the caramelization from the bottoms using the same technique.

2 Reveal The Sprinkles
Using a ruler as a guide and a serrated knife, carefully cut away the caramelization from all four sides of each layer, making sure to maintain its square shape.

3 Simple Syrup
Lay the cakes out on a clean work surface, and shower them with simple syrup. Let the syrup soak in fully before continuing.

4 First Layer
Place the first layer of cake onto a cake board on a lazy Susan. Place a dollop of vanilla buttercream onto the cake using the rubber spatula. Spread buttercream evenly onto the surface of the cake using a small offset spatula.

5 Crispy Cakefetti Square
Carefully, place a crispy cakefetti square layer on top of the first layer of cake. It is slightly larger than the trimmed cake below, so make sure the overhang is even on all four sides.

6 Spread It
Spread an even layer of vanilla buttercream onto the surface of the crispy funfetti square.

7 Second Layer
Place the second layer of cake on top and make sure it lines up with the bottom layer of cake. Spread buttercream evenly onto the surface of the cake using a small offset spatula.

8 Crispy Cakefetti Square
Place a second layer of crispy cakefetti square on top. Repeating the process, spread an even layer of vanilla buttercream onto the surface.

recipe continues

TOOLS

Ruler	Lazy Susan	3 parchment piping bags
Serrated knife	Rubber spatula	Bench scraper
Lil Squeeze	Small offset spatula	Chefs knife
12-inch square cake board	3 small bowls	Silicone pastry brush

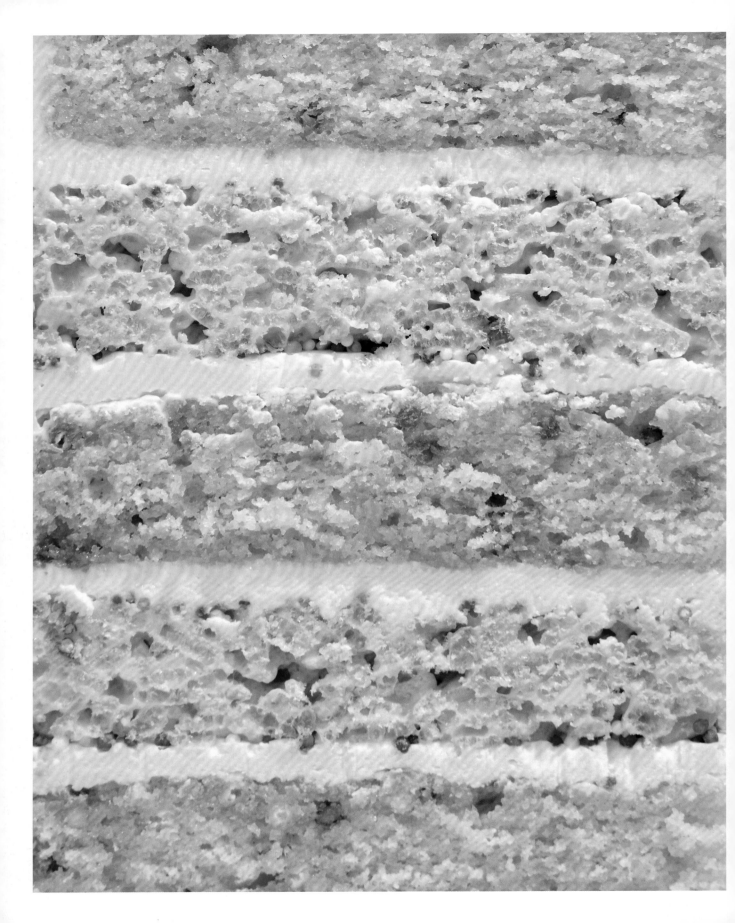

yo's tip!

You'll need to make 2 batches of cakefetti squares, the first batch will makes two 8-inch square thin layers to put in your cake. The second batch can be pressed into just one 8-inch pan and cut into squares to top your cake.

9 Top It Off
Place the final layer of cakefetti cake on top. Use a ruler held upright against the sides of the cake to make sure the layers line up.

10 Icing on the cake
Ice the cake using the small offset spatula, spreading buttercream into the horizontal grooves in the cake on all four sides. Crumb coat the top of the cake.

11 Smooth It Out
Use a bench scraper to smooth away any excess buttercream on the sides of the cake, partially exposing the crispy cakefetti treats. Pull the excess buttercream that has gathered along the top edge in toward the center of the cake, and smooth the top surface. Transfer the cake to the fridge to chill.

12 Get Colorful
While the cake chills, fill three bowls each with ¼ cup of buttercream. Tint each bowl of buttercream with pink, purple or orange gel color. Stir the gel color in a drop at a time until you reach the desired hue. Fill each parchment piping bag with a different color of buttercream.

13 Pipe It
Remove the cake from the fridge and pipe random horizontal lines of the tinted buttercream on all four sides. Use a small offset spatula to lightly smooth the lines of buttercream along the sides of the cake.

14 Drag It
Using the bench scraper, drag the colored buttercream across the sides of the cake in one direction.

15 Cut Cubes
Cut the thick crispy cakefetti square into 16 even cubes with a ruler and chef's knife.

16 Decorate It
Brush the sides of each marshmallow with piping gel. Coat each marshmallow with colored sanding sugar, 6 in pink and 6 in purple.

17 Finishing Touch
Top the cake with crispy cakefetti cubes and sugared marshmallows. Top cake with rainbow sprinkles.

crispy cakefetti squares

• 2 (8-INCH) SQUARES & 16 (2-INCH) SQUARES •

½ cup rainbow sprinkles
¼ cup (½ stick) unsalted butter
1 package (400g) mini
marshmallows

1 teaspoon pure
vanilla extract
6 cups puffed rice cereal

TOOLS
2 (8-inch) square cake pans,
lined
with parchment paper
Large saucepan
Wooden spoon

1 Add 2 tablespoons of sprinkles to the bottom of each prepared pan.

2 Melt the butter in the saucepan over medium-high heat. Add the mini marshmallows and stir, allowing the marshmallows to melt slowly.

3 When the marshmallows are almost completely melted (you should still see a few lumps), remove the saucepan from the heat and add the vanilla, stirring quickly.

4 Add the puffed rice cereal and stir until coated.

5 Divide the mixture between the two pans. Press the crispy cereal treats down firmly and evenly in each pan.

6 Sprinkle another 2 tablespoons of sprinkles on top of each pan of crispy treats, and press them in gently.

7 Allow the squares to set fully at room temperature.

yo's tip!

Butter or wet your hands before pressing the crispy mixture in the pans. This will stop it from sticking to your hands.

CAKE No.

two

movie night cake

HERE'S WHAT YOU'LL NEED TO PREP

Cake layers

Chocolate Cake
rounds 236

Syrup

Simple Syrup 256

Frosting

Vanilla
Buttercream 260

Fillings

Movie Night Snack
Discs 218

Candy coated
chocolate peanuts

Toppings

Candy coated
chocolate peanuts

Popped buttered
popcorn

movie night cake

— PREP IT! —

- 2 (8-inch) Chocolate Cake rounds (page 236) 1 recipe
- Simple Syrup (page 256)
- Vanilla Buttercream (page 260)
- yellow gel food coloring
- 2 Movie Night Snack Discs (page 218)
- 16 candy coated chocolate peanuts
- 2 cups popped buttered popcorn
- 2 ounces white chocolate, melted

LAYER UP!

1 Level Up & Layer Up
Remove the two cakes from their pans and peel off the parchment. Set the cakes right side up, and level them using a ruler and serrated knife. Cut each cake into two layers, for a total of four layers.

2 Simple Syrup
Lay the cakes out on a clean work surface, and shower them with simple syrup. Let the syrup soak in fully before continuing.

3 Color It
Measure 1½ cups of buttercream and place in a small bowl. Stir in the yellow gel color a drop at a time until you reach the desired hue.

4 First Layer
Place the first layer of cake onto a cake board on a lazy Susan. Place a dollop of buttercream onto the cake using the rubber spatula. Use a small offset spatula to smooth the buttercream around the sides of the cake. Then, pull the excess inward toward the center.

5 Movie Night Snack
Carefully, place a movie night snack disc on top. Spread a thin layer of buttercream onto the surface.

6 Second Layer
Place a second layer of chocolate cake on top.

7 Fill It
Fill one piping bag fitted with a #805 tip with the yellow buttercream. Fill the second bag, fitted with the same tip, with the same amount of vanilla buttercream.

8 Pipe It
Pipe a fence of yellow buttercream onto the surface of the cake around the edge. Switch to the white buttercream piping bag, and pipe a ring just inside the fence of yellow buttercream.

recipe continues

TOOLS

Ruler	Lazy Susan	2 piping bags
Serrated knife	Rubber spatula	2 #805 piping tips
Lil Squeeze	Small bowl	Parchment piping bag
12-inch round cake board	Small offset spatula	

9 Switch It Up
Continue to alternate piping bags, creating a bullseye pattern, on the surface of the cake, until you pipe a final dot in the center.

10 Third Layer
Place a third layer of chocolate cake on top. Use a small offset spatula to spread buttercream onto the surface. Smooth the buttercream around the sides of the cake. Then, pull the excess inward toward the center.

11 Movie Night Snack
Place a second movie night snack disc on top, and spread a thin layer of buttercream on top.

12 Top It Off
Place the final layer of chocolate cake on top, and ice it with buttercream, in the same manner as the previous layers.

13 Decorate It
Arrange a ring of 16 candy coated peanuts around the top edge of the cake.

14 Finishing Touch
Fill the parchment piping bag with the melted white chocolate. Build a mound of buttered popcorn in the center of the top of the cake. Use the white chocolate as glue to help the mound stay together.

movie night snack discs

• MAKES 2 (8-INCH) ROUNDS •

¼ cup (½ stick) unsalted butter

1 package (400g) mini marshmallows

5 cups popped popcorn

2 cups salted crinkle chips

1 cup candy-coated chocolate peanuts

TOOLS

Large saucepan

Wooden spoon

2 (8-inch) round cake pans, lined with parchment paper

1 Melt the butter in the saucepan over medium-high heat. Add the mini marshmallows and stir, allowing the marshmallows to melt slowly.

2 When the marshmallows are almost completely melted (you should still see a few lumps), remove the saucepan from heat.

3 Add the popcorn and chips and stir until coated.

4 Divide the mixture between the two pans, sprinkling in ½ cup of the candy-coated chocolate peanuts as you go. Press the mixture down firmly and evenly in each pan.

5 Allow the discs to set fully at room temperature.

CAKE N°
three

pink lemonade cake

HERE'S WHAT YOU'LL NEED TO PREP

Cake layers

Lemon Cake rounds 245

Pink Vanilla Cake rounds 246

Syrup

Lemon Simple Syrup 258

Frosting

Lemon Buttercream 263

Fillings

Lemon creme-filled wafers

Raspberry creme-filled wafers

Raspberries

Toppings

Lemon Tart 226

Isomalt Ice Cubes 225

Raspberries

Rock candy

Candy straw

pink lemonade cake

— PREP IT! —

- 1 (8-inch) Lemon Cake round (page 245) ½ recipe

- 2 (8-inch) Pink Vanilla Cake rounds (page 246) 1 recipe

- Lemon Simple Syrup (page 258)

- Lemon Buttercream (page 263)

- 30 Lemon creme-filled wafers (small squares), divided

- 1½ pints raspberries

- 30 Raspberry creme-filled wafers (small squares)

- Lemon Tart (page 226)

- 6 sticks rock candy, chopped

- Isomalt Ice Cubes, optional (page 225)

- candy straw, optional

LAYER UP!

1 Level Up & Layer Up
Remove all three cakes from their pans and peel off the parchment. Set the cakes right side up, and level them using a ruler and serrated knife. Flip the cakes over and remove the caramelization from the bottoms using the same technique.

2 Trim It
Place an 8-inch round cake pan upside down on top of one cake. Use a small serrated knife to trim the caramelization away from the side of the cake, inserting the knife straight down into the cake, and cutting around the template. Repeat with the other two layers.

3 Simple Syrup
Lay the cakes out on a clean work surface, and shower them with lemon simple syrup. Once the syrup has absorbed, flip all three layers over and shower the other side. Let the syrup soak in fully before continuing.

4 Spread It
Place each layer of cake onto its own cake board. Working one at a time ,on a lazy Susan, place a dollop of lemon buttercream onto the surface of one layer using a rubber spatula. Use a small offset spatula to smooth the lemon buttercream over the surface of the cake.

5 Crumb Coat & Chill
Crumb coat the sides of the layer. Then, pull the excess buttercream inward toward the center on top of the cake. Transfer the cake to the fridge to chill for 20 minutes.

6 One More Time
Repeat steps 4 and 5 with the two remaining layers and place them in the fridge to chill.

recipe continues

TOOLS		
Ruler	Small serrated knife	Lazy Susan
Serrated knife	Lil Squeeze	Rubber Spatula
7-inch round cake pan	3 (12-inch) round cake boards	Small offset spatula

LEMON
ADE
CAKE
21¢
SLICE

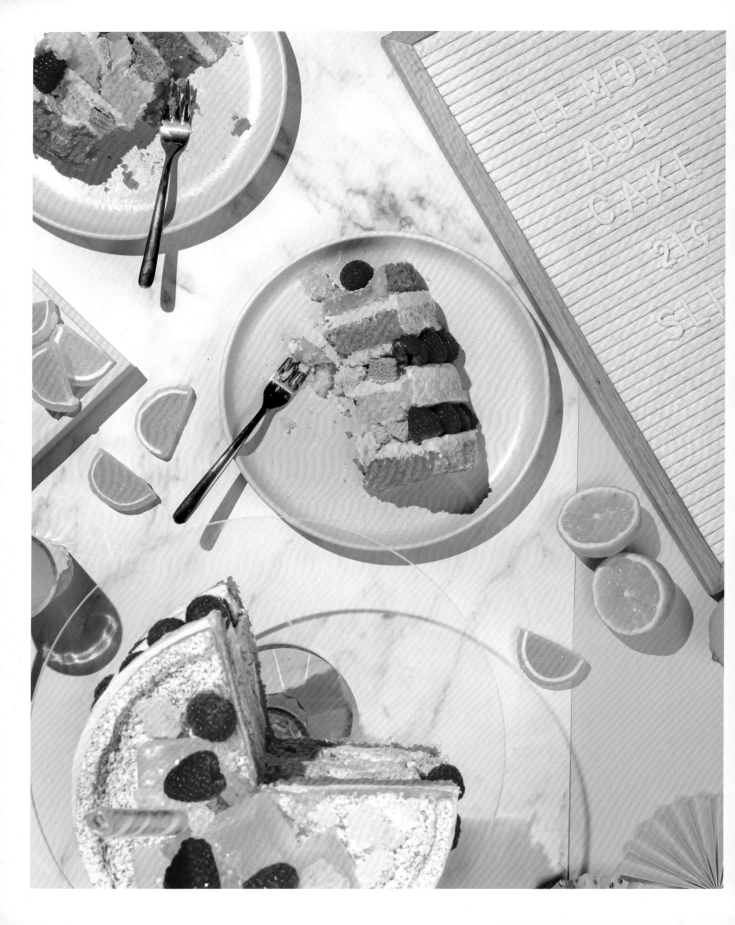

LEMON
ADE
CAKE
21¢
SLI

7 First Layer
Remove a pink iced layer of cake from the fridge. Line up the lemon wafer squares on the surface, making sure to leave a ½" border around the top edge of the cake.

8 Spread It
Spread an even layer of lemon buttercream onto the wafers.

9 Get In Formation
Arrange a ring of raspberries along the edge of the cake making sure that the pointy end of each berry faces up.

10 Second Layer
Carefully, place the chilled plain lemon iced cake on top of the buttercream and raspberries, making sure it lines up with the first layer.

11 One More Time
Repeat steps 7 to 9, this time lining up the raspberry wafer squares on the layer.

12 Top It Off
Carefully, place the final chilled pink iced cake on top of the buttercream and raspberries, making sure it lines up with the layers below.

13 Finishing Touch
Center the lemon tart on top, and decorate with the rock candy, isomalt cubes and candy straw, if using. Add a few fresh raspberries to the top of the cake to resemble the top of a tall, cool glass of lemonade.

isomalt ice cubes

1 cup isomalt crystals

TOOLS
Small heavy bottom saucepan
Wooden spoon
Candy thermometer
Silicone ice cube mold

1 Combine the isomalt with ¼ cup of water in the saucepan.

2 Place over medium heat and allow the crystals to dissolve. Bring the mixture to 320°F.

3 Carefully pour the isomalt into the cavities of the silicone ice cube tray. Pour slowly, little by little, and allow the bubbles to settle before continuing to pour.

4 Allow the isomalt cubes to cool and set completely before removing from the mold.

lemon shortbread tart

• MAKES 1 (8-INCH) ROUND TART •

PASTRY

1 cup all-purpose flour, sifted

½ cup (1 stick) unsalted butter, room temperature

¼ cup icing sugar

¼ teaspoon salt

FILLING

1 cup granulated sugar

1 tablespoon all-purpose flour

½ tablespoon lemon zest (1 lemon)

¾ teaspoon baking soda

2 large eggs

¼ cup + 1 tablespoon fresh lemon juice (2 lemons)

icing sugar, for dusting

TOOLS

8-inch round tart pan with removable bottom

Stand mixer with paddle attachment

Small cake pan or glass with a flat base

Baking tray, lined with parchment paper or a silicone mat

Medium bowl

Whisk

Sieve

1 Make the crust: Mix the flour, butter, icing sugar and salt together in a stand mixer fitted with a paddle attachment, until you achieve a crumb-like consistency.

2 Press the mixture along the sides and bottom of the tart pan, making sure the sides are even. Use a smaller cake pan or glass with a flat base to press the crumbs into the bottom.

3 Transfer the shell to the fridge and chill for 30 minutes. Preheat oven to 350°F.

4 Place the tart pan onto the baking tray and bake for 15 minutes. Allow to cool completely.

5 Make the filling: Meanwhile, whisk the sugar, flour, lemon zest, and baking soda together in a medium bowl.

6 Add the eggs and lemon juice and continue to whisk. The mixture will become frothy. Pour half of the mixture into the cooled crust, allow it to settle, then pour in the rest.

7 Bake the tart for 20 minutes, carefully rotating the tray halfway through. Allow the tart to cool completely before removing from the pan.

8 If desired, dust the entire surface of the tart with icing sugar.

lemon curd

• MAKES 1½ CUPS •

½ tablespoon lemon zest
(from about 1 lemon)
½ cup granulated sugar
5 large egg yolks

1 large egg
⅓ cup fresh lemon juice
(from 2 to 4 lemons)
2 tablespoons (¼ stick)
unsalted butter

TOOLS
Small saucepan
Whisk
Large stainless steel bowl
Wooden spoon
Medium bowl

1 Fill the saucepan half-way with water and place on the stove until simmering.

2 Whisk together lemon zest and sugar in a large stainless steel bowl. Add egg yolks and egg and whisk to combine. Finally, whisk in the lemon juice.

3 Place the bowl onto the saucepan over the simmering water. Let the curd thicken over medium heat, whisking from time to time. Cook for 20 to 25 minutes or until the curd is thick.

4 Remove the bowl from the heat and add the butter. Let the butter melt and then stir it into the lemon curd with a wooden spoon.

5 Transfer the curd to a medium bowl. Press plastic wrap directly on top of curd. Allow curd to cool completely, and place in the fridge. Use this curd to flavor your buttercream.

yo's tip!

You can freeze lemon curd. Place it in an airtight container with a layer of plastic directly on the surface of the curd. Thaw in the fridge before use.

pink lemonade cake
220

Swap the wafers for your favorite lemon sandwich cookie.

cakefetti cake
204

Try your favorite color combination on the outside of this cake for a different look every time.

movie night cake
212

Top this cake with a pile of caramel popcorn if you have an extra-sweet tooth.

core
recipes

· · · · · · · · · · ·

layer up

This chart is your ultimate guide to layering up. Always check this chart to make sure your baking the right amount of cake.

CINNAMON BUN CAKE (PAGE 34)

=

CAKE SIZE
3 (8-inch) rounds

CAKE RECIPE
Cinnamon Bun (page 242)

№ OF RECIPES
1½ batches

CHOCOLATE PEANUT BUTTER CAKE (PAGE 76)

=

CAKE SIZE
2 (8-inch) rounds

CAKE RECIPE
Chocolate (page 236)

№ OF RECIPES
1

COFFEE & DONUTS CAKE (PAGE 42)

=

CAKE SIZE
1 (8-inch) round

CAKE RECIPE
Chocolate
(page 236)

№ OF RECIPES
½

CAKE SIZE
2 (8-inch) rounds

CAKE RECIPE
Vanilla
(page 240)

№ OF RECIPES
1

CARAMEL CONE CAKE (PAGE 90)

=

CAKE SIZE
3 (8-inch) rounds

CAKE RECIPE
Marble (page 246)

№ OF RECIPES
1½

LEMON BLUEBERRY PANCAKE CAKE (PAGE 48)

=

CAKE SIZE
2 (8-inch) rounds

CAKE RECIPE
Lemon (page 245)

№ OF RECIPES
1

TROPICAL UPSIDE DOWN CAKE (PAGE 98)

=

CAKE SIZE
3 (8-inch) rounds

CAKE RECIPE
Coconut Pineapple
(page 253)

№ OF RECIPES
1

CHOCOLATE COCONUT CAKE (PAGE 62)

=

CAKE SIZE
2 (8-inch) rounds

CAKE RECIPE
Chocolate Coconut
(page 238)

№ OF RECIPES
1

VELVET CHEESECAKE BROWNIE CAKE (PAGE 104)

=

CAKE SIZE
2 (9-inch) rounds

CAKE RECIPE
Red Velvet (page 254)

№ OF RECIPES
1

CHOCOLATE MINT CAKE (PAGE 70)

=

CAKE SIZE
2 (8-inch) rounds

CAKE RECIPE
Chocolate (page 236)

№ OF RECIPES
1

CHOCOLATE CHIP COOKIE CAKE (PAGE 116)

=

CAKE SIZE
2 (8-inch) rounds

CAKE RECIPE
Chocolate Chip
(page 242)

№ OF RECIPES
1

COOKIES & CREAM CAKE (PAGE 126)

=

CAKE SIZE
1 (8-inch) round

CAKE RECIPE
Black Chocolate (page 238)

№ OF RECIPES
½

CAKE SIZE
2 (8-inch) rounds

CAKE RECIPE
Cookies & Cream (page 243)

№ OF RECIPES
1

APPLE PIE CAKE (PAGE 170)

=

CAKE SIZE
2 (8-inch) rounds

CAKE RECIPE
Spice (page 247)

№ OF RECIPES
1

S'MORE CAKE (PAGE 132)

=

CAKE SIZE
1 (8-inch) square

CAKE RECIPE
Chocolate (page 236)

№ OF RECIPES
½

CAKE SIZE
2 (8-inch) squares

CAKE RECIPE
Graham Crusted Chocolate (page 239)

№ OF RECIPES
1

BANOFFEE PIE CAKE (PAGE 182)

=

CAKE SIZE
2 (8-inch) rounds

CAKE RECIPE
Graham Crusted Banana (page 249)

№ OF RECIPES
1

BAKLAVA CAKE (PAGE 142)

=

CAKE SIZE
3 (8-inch) squares

CAKE RECIPE
Vanilla (page 240)

№ OF RECIPES
1½

KEY LIME PIE CAKE (PAGE 190)

=

CAKE SIZE
4 (8-inch) rounds

CAKE RECIPE
Caramel Biscuit Crusted Lime (page 244)

№ OF RECIPES
1½

CHOCOLATE HAZELNUT CAKE (PAGE 150)

=

CAKE SIZE
3 (8-inch) rounds

CAKE RECIPE
Chocolate (page 236)

№ OF RECIPES
1

CAKEFETTI CAKE (PAGE 204)

=

CAKE SIZE
3 (8-inch) squares

CAKE RECIPE
Cakefetti (page 245)

№ OF RECIPES
1½

FALL HARVEST CAKE (PAGE 158)

=

CAKE SIZE
3 (8-inch) rounds

CAKE RECIPE
Gingersnap Crusted Carrot Walnut (page 251)

№ OF RECIPES
1

MOVIE NIGHT CAKE (PAGE 212)

=

CAKE SIZE
2 (8-inch) rounds

CAKE RECIPE
Chocolate (page 236)

№ OF RECIPES
1

PINK LEMONADE CAKE (PAGE 220)

=

CAKE SIZE
1 (8-inch) round

CAKE RECIPE
Lemon (page 245)

№ OF RECIPES
½

CAKE SIZE
2 (8-inch) rounds

CAKE RECIPE
Pink Vanilla (page 246)

№ OF RECIPES
1

chocolate cake

This chocolate cake is my go-to recipe. It's moist, delicious, and sturdy. I've been making this chocolate cake recipe for twenty years, with a few tweaks here and there, and it has never let me down. Whether it's smothered with buttercream or dripping with ganache, it's delicious.

2¾ cups all-purpose flour

2 teaspoons baking powder

1½ teaspoons baking soda

1 teaspoon salt

1 cup Dutch-processed cocoa powder

1 cup (2 sticks) unsalted butter, room temperature

2½ cups granulated sugar

4 large eggs, room temperature

TOOLS

2 (8-inch) round cake pans

Sieve

Medium saucepan

Medium bowl

Medium heatproof bowl

Whisk

Stand mixer with paddle attachment

Rubber spatula

Metal cooling rack

Small straight spatula

Cake tester

1 Preheat oven to 350°F. Line the bottom of each cake pan with parchment paper.

2 Sift together flour, baking powder, baking soda, and salt into a medium bowl. Set aside.

3 Put the cocoa powder in a medium heatproof bowl. In a saucepan bring 3 cups of water to a boil, then carefully measure exactly 2 cups and pour over the cocoa powder. Whisk until completely smooth. Set aside and allow to cool slightly.

4 In the bowl of a stand mixer fitted with the paddle attachment, cream butter and sugar on medium speed until light and fluffy, about 8 minutes.

5 Add the eggs, two at a time, beating until each addition is incorporated before adding the next. Scrape down the sides of the bowl with a spatula when necessary.

6 Add the flour mixture in four parts, alternating with the warm cocoa mixture in three parts. Beat just until each addition is incorporated before adding the next; do not overmix.

7 Pour the batter into the prepared pans. Bake until a toothpick inserted in the center comes out clean, about 55 minutes, rotating the pans halfway through.

8 Transfer cakes to a metal cooling rack and allow to cool completely in the pans. Cover tightly with plastic wrap and refrigerate overnight.

9 To remove, loosen the edges with a small straight spatula. Invert the pans to remove the cakes and peel off the parchment.

recipe continues

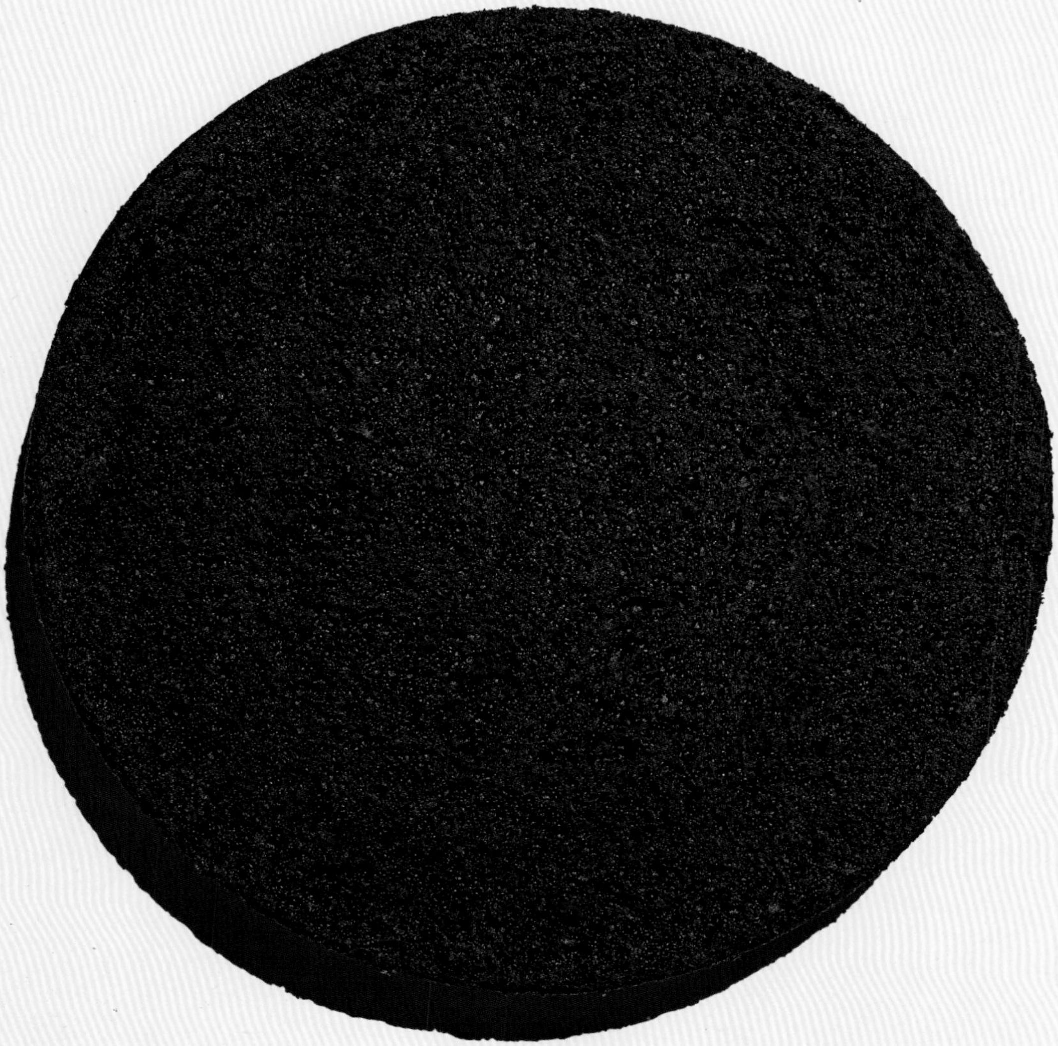

ingredients	½ recipe	1 recipe	1½ recipes
all-purpose	1⅓ cups	2¾ cups	4 cups + 2 tbsp
baking powder	1 teaspoon	2 teaspoons	1 tablespoon
baking soda	¾ teaspoon	1½ teaspoons	2¼ teaspoons
table salt	½ teaspoon	1 teaspoon	1½ teaspoon
cocoa powder	½ cup	1 cup	1½ cups
boiling water	1 cup	2 cups	3 cups
unsalted butter	½ cup (1 stick)	1 cup (2 sticks)	1½ cups (3 sticks)
sugar	1¼ cups	2½ cups	3¾ cups
large eggs	2	4	6

CHOCOLATE COCONUT CAKE

1 cup shredded, unsweetened coconut

Add the coconut to the chocolate batter
as a final step before dividing the batter
between the pans.

BLACK CHOCOLATE CAKE

1 tablespoon black gel food coloring

While preparing a ½ recipe of chocolate
cake batter, add the black gel food
coloring to the cocoa and hot water
mixture in step 3.

GRAHAM CRUSTED CHOCOLATE CAKE

3 cups graham crumbs

1 cup + 2 tablespoons unsalted butter, melted

½ cup granulated sugar

1 Before preparing one recipe of chocolate cake batter, create the cookie crust base. Stir together the graham crumbs, melted butter, and sugar until combined. Divide the mixture evenly between the two prepared pans.

2 Use a smaller cake pan or a drinking glass with a flat base to press the mixture down and compress. Place the pans in the fridge, and prepare your batter.

vanilla cake

I am really proud of this vanilla cake.
I love its buttery, sweet flavor and its texture.
It is perfect for simple cakes layered with
buttercream and toppings.

2½ cups all-purpose flour

2½ teaspoons baking powder

½ teaspoon salt

1 cup (2 sticks) unsalted butter,
room temperature

2 cups granulated sugar

1 teaspoon pure vanilla extract

4 large eggs, room temperature

1 cup whole milk, room
temperature

TOOLS

2 (8-inch) cake pans

Sieve

Medium bowl

Stand mixer with paddle
attachment

Rubber spatula

Metal cooling rack

Small straight spatula

Cake tester

1 Preheat oven to 350°F. Line the bottom of each cake pan with parchment paper.

2 Sift together flour, baking powder, and salt into a medium bowl. Set aside.

3 In the bowl of a stand mixer fitted with the paddle attachment, beat the butter, sugar, and vanilla on medium speed until light and fluffy, about 8 minutes.

4 Add the eggs, two at a time, beating until each addition is incorporated before adding the next. Scrape down the sides of the bowl with a spatula when necessary.

5 Add the flour mixture in four parts, alternating with the milk in three parts. Beat just until each addition is incorporated before adding the next; do not overmix.

6 Scrape the batter into the prepared pans and spread it so that it is smooth. Bake until a toothpick inserted in the center comes out clean, about 45 minutes, rotating the pans halfway through.

7 Transfer to a metal cooling rack and allow to cool completely in the pans. Cover tightly with plastic wrap and refrigerate overnight.

8 To remove, loosen the edges with a small straight spatula. Invert the pans to remove the cakes, and peel off the parchment.

recipe continues

ingredients	½ recipe	1 recipe	1½ recipe
all-purpose flour	1¼ cups	2½ cups	3¾ cups
baking powder	1¼ teaspoons	2½ teaspoons	3¾ teaspoons
table salt	¼ teaspoon	½ teaspoon	¾ teaspoon
unsalted butter	½ cup (1 stick)	1 cup (2 sticks)	1½ cups (3 sticks)
sugar	1 cup	2 cups	3 cups
pure vanilla extract	½ teaspoon	1 teaspoon	1½ teaspoon
large eggs	2	4	6
whole milk	½ cup	1 cup	1½ cups

CHOCOLATE CHIP CAKE ————————→

1½ cups mini chocolate chips

Add the mini chocolate chips into the batter at the end of step 5 of the vanilla cake batter recipe before diving the batter between the pans.

CINNAMON BUN CAKE

2 cups dark brown sugar, packed

¼ cup ground cinnamon

1½ cups (3 sticks) salted butter, melted

Stir the brown sugar and cinnamon into the melted butter. Divide the mixture evenly on top of three pans filled with vanilla cake batter. Swirl into the batter with a bamboo skewer, or a butter knife, before baking.

COOKIES & CREAM CAKE

2 cups chocolate cookie crumbs

⅓ cup granulated sugar

¾ cup (1½ sticks) unsalted butter, melted

2 cups chopped chocolate cookie sandwiches

1 Before preparing the cake batter, make the cookie crust base. Mix together the chocolate cookie crumbs, sugar and melted butter until combined. Divide the mixture evenly between the two prepared pans.

2 Use a smaller cake pan or a drinking glass with a flat base to press the mixture down to compress. Place the pans in the fridge, and prepare the batter.

3 Fold the chopped chocolate cookies into the batter in step 5 of the vanilla cake batter recipe. Divide the batter evenly between the two pans, and bake.

**CARAMEL BISCUIT CRUSTED
LIME CAKE**

**4 cups caramel biscuit crumbs
(about 64 cookies)**

¼ cup granulated sugar

**1½ cups (3 sticks) unsalted butter,
melted**

2 tablespoons lime zest

1 Before preparing the vanilla cake batter, make the cookie
crust base. Combine the caramel biscuit crumbs, melted butter,
and sugar together in a medium bowl. Divide the mixture evenly
between the two prepared pans. Use a smaller cake pan or
a drinking glass with a flat base to press the mixture down to
compress. Place the pans in the fridge, and prepare the batter.

2 Add the lime zest in step 3 when you are creaming the butter,
sugar, and vanilla together for the vanilla cake batter. Once your
batter is complete, divide it evenly amongst 4 pans on top of the
prepared crust.

CAKEFETTI CAKE

¾ cup rainbow sprinkles

Add the sprinkles into the batter in step 5 of the vanilla cake batter recipe dividing the batter amongst the pans.

LEMON CAKE

2 tablespoons lemon zest

Add the lemon zest in step 3 when you are creaming the butter, sugar, and vanilla together for the vanilla cake batter.

PINK VANILLA CAKE

1 tablespoon of neon pink gel food color

Add the gel food color in step 3 when you are creaming the butter, sugar, and vanilla together for the vanilla cake batter.

MARBLE CAKE

1½ batches vanilla batter (page 000)
1½ batches chocolate batter (page 000)

Prepare both cake batters. Divide the batters evenly amongst the three prepared cake pans, alternating large spoonfuls of chocolate and vanilla batter. Once all the batter is distributed, use a bamboo stick or butter knife to swirl the chocolate and vanilla by gently stirring the batter together in small circles. Be careful not to overmix as you don't want to blend the batters completely.

SPICE CAKE

¼ cup granulated sugar
1 teaspoon cinnamon
¼ teaspoon nutmeg

Whisk together sugar, cinnamon, and nutmeg. Prepare the vanilla cake batter. Divide half of the batter between the two prepared pans. Sprinkle the spice mixture evenly on top of both cakes, then top with the remaining batter. Smooth the top with a rubber spatula making sure the batter reaches the edge of the pan. Use a bamboo skewer, or butter knife, to swirl the spice mixture into the batter.

Banana cake

3¾ cups all-purpose flour

2¼ teaspoons baking powder

2¼ teaspoons baking soda

1½ teaspoon salt

**6 overripe bananas
(the skin should be bruised
and blackened)**

**1 cup + 2 tablespoons buttermilk,
room temperature**

**1½ cups (3 sticks) unsalted butter,
room temperature**

3 cups granulated sugar

1½ teaspoon pure vanilla extract

6 large eggs, room temperature

TOOLS

2 (8-inch) round cake pans

Sieve

2 medium bowls

Whisk

Potato masher

**Stand mixer with paddle
attachment**

Rubber spatula

Metal cooling rack

Small straight spatula

Cake tester

1 Preheat oven to 350°F. Line the bottom of each cake pan with parchment paper.

2 Sift the flour, baking powder, baking soda, and salt into a medium bowl and whisk together. Set aside.

3 Peel the bananas and place in a separate bowl. Mash them using your hands, or a potato masher. Whisk in ¾ cup of buttermilk. Set aside.

4 In the bowl of a stand mixer fitted with the paddle attachment, beat the butter, sugar and vanilla on medium speed, until light and fluffy, about 8 minutes

5 Add the eggs, two at a time, beating until each addition is incorporated before adding the next. Scrape down the sides of the bowl with a rubber spatula, when necessary.

6 Add the flour mixture in four parts, alternating with the banana buttermilk mixture in three parts. Beat just until each addition is incorporated before adding the next; do not overmix.

7 Pour the batter into the prepared pans. Bake until a toothpick inserted in the center comes out clean, about 55 minutes, rotating the pans halfway through.

8 Transfer to a metal cooling rack and allow to cool completely in the pans. Cover tightly with plastic wrap and refrigerate overnight. To release, loosen the edges of the cakes with a small straight spatula, invert the pans and peel off the parchment.

yo's tip!

If buttermilk is hard to find, you can make your own. Stir 1 teaspoon of distilled white or cider vinegar per cup of room temperature milk. Lets stand for 10 to 15 minutes until the milk has thickened.

GRAHAM CRUSTED
BANANA CAKE

3 cups graham cracker crumbs

½ cup granulated sugar

1 cup (2 sticks) + 2 tablespoons unsalted butter, melted

1 Before preparing the banana cake batter, create the cookie crust base. Mix together graham cracker crumbs, sugar and butter in a bowl.

2 Divide the mixture evenly between the two prepared pans.

3 Use a smaller cake pan or a drinking glass with a flat base to press the mixture down to compress.

4 Place the pans in the fridge while you prepare the cake batter.

5 Once your batter is complete, divide it evenly between 2 pans on top of the prepared crust.

carrot cake

2½ cups all-purpose flour

1 tablespoon baking powder

1 tablespoon baking soda

1 tablespoon cinnamon

1 teaspoon nutmeg

½ teaspoon salt

2½ cups light brown sugar, packed

1¼ cups whole pureed orange (approximately 3 small oranges)

5 large eggs, room temperature

1½ cups vegetable oil

2½ cups peeled, grated carrots

TOOLS

3 (8-inch) round cake pans

Sieve

Large bowl

Whisk

Food processor

Stand mixer with whisk attachment

Small straight spatula

Metal cooling rack

Cake tester

1 Preheat oven to 350°F. Line the bottom of each cake pan with parchment paper.

2 Sift the flour, baking powder, baking soda, cinnamon, nutmeg, and salt into a large bowl. Add in the golden brown sugar. Whisk to combine. Set aside.

3 Wash and dry the oranges. Cut the ends off each orange and cut into small pieces. Purée the oranges in a food processor or blender until smooth. Measure out the 1¼ cups you will need for this recipe and set aside.

4 In the bowl of a stand mixer fitted with the whisk attachment, whisk the puréed orange and eggs on high speed for 3 to 5 minutes.

5 Slowly pour in the vegetable oil along the side of the mixing bowl, still whisking the orange and egg mixture on high speed. I recommend using the guard for your stand mixer if you have one!

6 As you pour the oil in slowly but surely, you will notice this mixture will really thicken up. When you've finished adding the oil, continue whisking the mixture for an additional 5 minutes.

7 Once oil is combined, remove the guard from the mixer and turn it down to low speed. Start adding the dry ingredients, scraping down the sides with a rubber spatula occasionally. Be careful not to overmix.

8 Still on low speed, add in the grated carrots.

9 Divide the batter evenly into the prepared pans. Bake for 1 hour or until a toothpick or cake tester comes out clean.

10 Transfer cakes to a metal cooling rack and allow to cool completely in the pans. Cover tightly with plastic wrap and refrigerate overnight. To release, loosen the edges of the cakes with a small straight spatula. Invert the pans to remove the cakes, and peel off the parchment.

yo's tip!

If the oranges you have selected are really juicy, add more rind from another orange to your food processor. You want the orange purée to be thick.

GINGERSNAP CRUSTED WALNUT CARROT CAKE

3 cups gingersnap crumbs

½ cup granulated sugar

1 cup (2 sticks) + 2 tablespoons unsalted butter, melted

1 Before preparing the carrot cake batter, create the cookie crust base. Mix together gingersnap crumbs, sugar and butter, in a bowl.

2 Divide the mixture amongst the 3 prepared pans.

3 Use a smaller cake pan or a drinking glass with a flat base to press the mixture down to compress.

4 Place the pans on the fridge while you prepare the cake batter.

5 Once your batter is complete, fold in the walnuts. Divide the batter evenly amongst the 3 pans on top of the prepared crust.

coconut cake

3 cups all-purpose flour

1 tablespoon baking powder

1 tablespoon baking soda

1 cup sweetened, desiccated or shredded coconut

1 cup (2 sticks) salted butter, room temperature

2 cups granulated sugar

2 teaspoons pure vanilla extract

4 large egg whites, room temperature

4 large eggs, room temperature

2⅓ cups unsweetened coconut milk (a bit less than 1½ [13.5 ounce] cans)

TOOLS

3 (8-inch) round cake pans

Sieve

Medium bowl

Whisk

Stand mixer with paddle attachment

Small straight spatula

Metal cooling rack

Cake tester

1 Preheat oven to 350°F. Line the bottom of each cake pan with parchment paper.

2 Sift the flour, baking powder and baking soda into a medium bowl. Whisk in the coconut. Set aside.

3 In the bowl of a stand mixer fitted with the paddle attachment, beat the butter, sugar, and vanilla on medium speed until light and fluffy, about 8 minutes

4 Add the egg whites and whole eggs, two at a time, beating until each addition is incorporated before adding the next. Scrape down the sides of the bowl with a spatula, when necessary.

5 Add the flour mixture in four parts, alternating with the coconut milk in three parts, beating just until each addition is incorporated before adding the next; do not overmix.

6 Pour the batter into the prepared pans. Bake until a toothpick inserted in the center comes out clean, about 55 minutes, rotating the pans halfway through.

7 Transfer to a metal cooling rack and allow to cool completely in the pans. Cover tightly with plastic wrap and refrigerate overnight. To release, loosen the edges of the cakes with a small straight spatula. Invert the pans to remove the cakes, and peel off the parchment.

PINEAPPLE COCONUT UPSIDE DOWN CAKE

3 whole, fresh pineapples, peeled and cored

¾ cup (1½ sticks) unsalted butter, melted

1½ cup light brown sugar, packed

1 jar maraschino cherries, drained

TOOLS

Chef's knife

Silicone pastry brush

Cutting board

1 Slice the cored pineapples into ½-inch slices. Cut ¼ out of each slice, so that they look like the letter "C."

2 Pour ¼ cup of melted butter into each of the prepared pans. Spread it evenly on the surface of the parchment paper with a silicone pastry brush.

3 Sprinkle ½ cup of brown sugar into each pan, distributing it evenly on top of the butter.

4 Arrange the pineapple slices in each pan, fanning them within the circle. Each pan should hold 6 to 7 slices.

5 Place a maraschino cherry into the center of each pineapple slice and in the open pockets along the edge of the pan.

6 Divide the coconut cake batter evenly amongst the 3 pans, pouring it carefully onto the fruit layer you just created. Add 10 minutes to baking time.

red velvet cake

4 cups all-purpose flour

1 tablespoon cocoa powder (not Dutch-processed)

2 teaspoons salt

1 cup (2 sticks) unsalted butter, room temperature

⅓ cup vegetable oil

3 cups granulated sugar

1½ teaspoons pure vanilla extract

2 tablespoons red gel food coloring

4 large eggs, room temperature

2 cups buttermilk, room temperature

2 teaspoons baking soda

2 teaspoons cider vinegar

TOOLS

2 (9-inch) round cake pans

Sieve

Whisk

Stand mixer with paddle attachment

Rubber spatula

Metal cooling rack

Small straight spatula

Small bowl

Medium bowl

Cake tester

1 Preheat oven to 350°F. Line the bottom of each cake pan with parchment paper.

2 Sift the flour, cocoa, and salt into a medium bowl and whisk together. Set aside.

3 In the bowl of a stand mixer fitted with the paddle attachment, beat the butter, oil, sugar, and vanilla on medium speed until well combined, about 5 minutes.

4 Add the red gel food coloring and beat until the batter is evenly colored. Scrape the sides and bottom of the bowl to make sure the mixture is even and doesn't have streaks.

5 Add the eggs, two at a time, beating until each addition is incorporated before adding the next. Scrape down the sides of the bowl with a spatula when necessary.

6 Add the flour mixture in four parts, alternating with the buttermilk in three parts, beating just until each addition is incorporated before adding the next. Do not overmix.

7 In a small bowl, combine the baking soda and cider vinegar. With the mixer running, immediately add the mixture to the batter. Beat for 10 seconds.

8 Scrape the batter into the prepared pans and spread it so that it is smooth on top. Bake until a toothpick inserted in the center comes out clean, about 45 minutes to 55 minutes, rotating the pans halfway through.

9 Transfer cakes to a metal cooling rack and allow to cool completely in the pans. Cover tightly with plastic wrap and refrigerate overnight. To release, loosen the edges of the cakes with a small straight spatula. Invert the pans to remove the cakes, and peel off the parchment.

crumb crusts

Crumb crusts are very popular for pies and bars, but I love adding them to cake layers. I have to cake-ify everything! The crusts add unexpected flavor and texture within the cake that everyone is sure to enjoy.

GRAHAM CRACKER
CRUMBS

CHOCOLATE
COOKIE CRUMBS

GINGERSNAP
CRUMBS

CARAMEL
BISCUIT CRUMBS

simple syrup

If you've seen just one episode of How To Cake It, you've seen me use simple syrup. I sprinkle this syrup on all my cakes to keep them moist throughout assembly, decoration, and refrigeration. Simple syrups are also an impactful way to add flavor.

• **MAKES 1½ CUPS** •

1 cup water

1 cup granulated sugar

TOOLS

Small saucepan

Small bowl

Wooden spoon

1 Pour the water into the saucepan and pour the sugar on top. Bring to a boil over medium heat. Stir to make sure the sugar is completely dissolved.

2 Pour the syrup into a bowl and let cool completely.

recipe continues

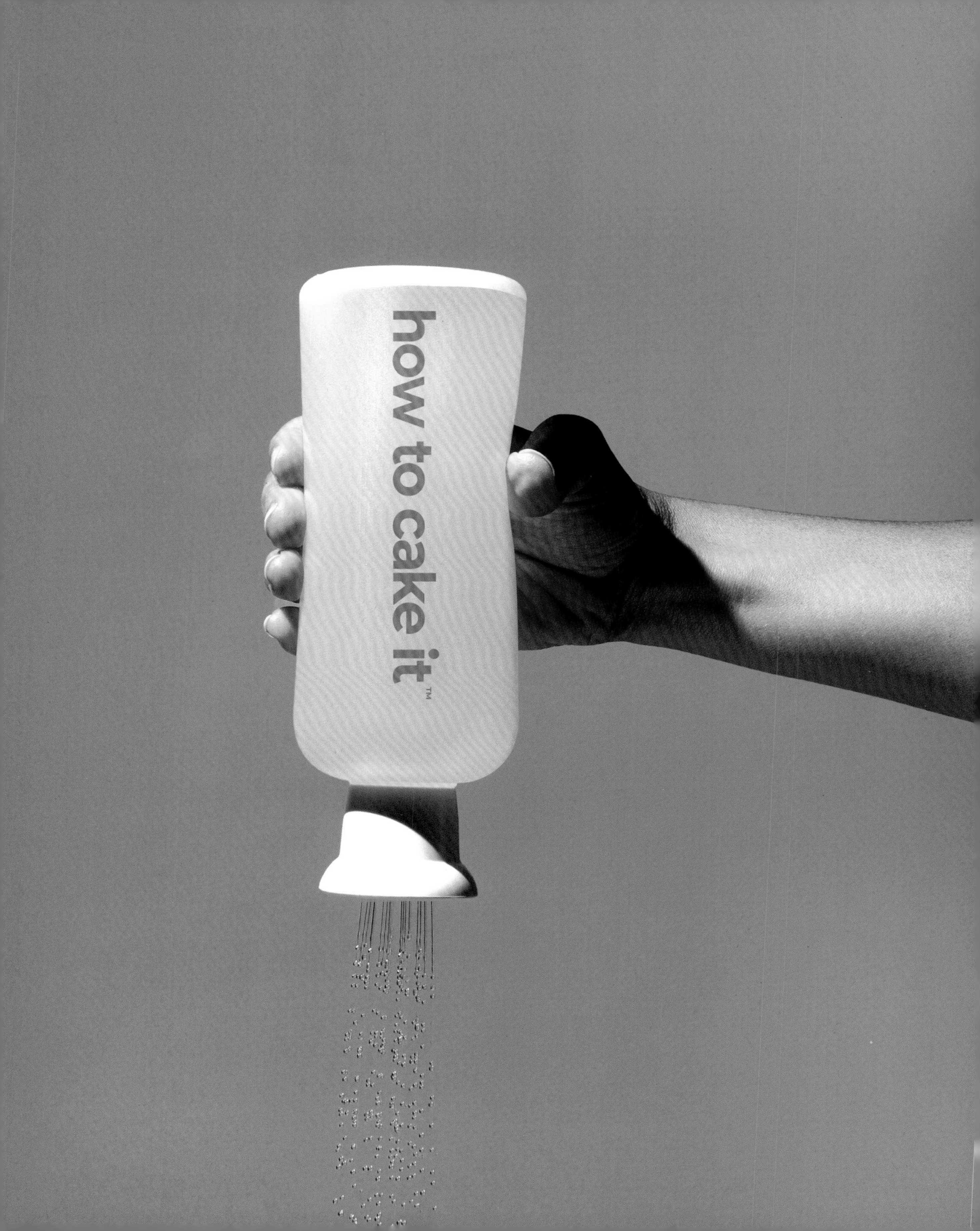
how to cake it™

LIME SIMPLE SYRUP

Replace ½ cup of the water with ½ cup fresh lime juice.

LEMON SIMPLE SYRUP

Replace ½ cup of the water with ½ cup fresh lemon juice.

APPLE SPICE SIMPLE SYRUP

Replace ½ cup of the water with ½ cup apple juice. Add a small cinnamon stick and 3 cloves.

Yo's tip!

To create these flavored simple syrups, apply these changes to the core simple syrup recipe (page 256).

COFFEE SIMPLE SYRUP

Replace 1 cup water with 1 cup strong-brewed coffee.

BROWN SUGAR SIMPLE SYRUP

Replace 1 cup granulated sugar with 1 cup packed dark brown sugar.

HONEY SIMPLE SYRUP

Replace ½ cup of the granulated sugar with ½ cup good-quality liquid honey.

PINEAPPLE RUM SIMPLE SYRUP

Replace ½ cup of the water with ½ cup pineapple juice. Add ¼ cup of rum after the syrup has boiled.

COCONUT SIMPLE SYRUP

Replace 1 cup water with 1 cup coconut water.

vanilla buttercream

This is an Italian meringue buttercream, which is the trickiest recipe to master but well worth the effort. I failed my first few attempts at this recipe so don't get discouraged. Even though I've made this thousands of times I always use a thermometer and never walk away. Temperature and timing are everything. This is my go to buttercream, because it's light and yummy yet not to sweet.

• MAKES 4½ CUPS •

1¾ cups granulated sugar

½ cup water

8 large egg whites, room temperature

2 cups (4 sticks) unsalted butter, cut into tablespoon-size pieces, room temperature

1 teaspoon pure vanilla extract

TOOLS

Medium saucepan

Candy thermometer

Stand mixer with whisk attachment

Rubber spatula

1 In a small saucepan, combine the sugar and water. Place over medium heat and bring to a boil. Clip a candy thermometer to the side of the pan.

2 While the sugar syrup is heating, put the egg whites in the bowl of a stand mixer fitted with the whisk attachment.

3 When the syrup reaches 230°F on the candy thermometer, begin to whip the egg whites on medium-high speed. Whip until the egg whites are stiff. The idea is to get to this stage by the time the syrup reaches 240°F so that you can then move on to the next step.

4 When the syrup reaches 240°F, immediately remove the pan from the heat and, with the mixer running, pour the syrup into the egg whites in a very thin stream. Pour the syrup between the side of the bowl and the whisk attachment. Be very careful; this syrup is HOT! You do not want it to hit the whisk attachment and splash you.

5 Whip the meringue at high speed until thick and glossy and the bowl is no longer warm on the outside, about 8 to 12 minutes. Allow the mixture to cool down completely. When you touch the side of the bowl, it shouldn't feel hot. This may take longer for you, or it may happen faster.

6 With the mixer running, add the butter, a piece at a time until all you have added all the butter. Scrape down the sides of the bowl with a spatula occasionally.

7 After all the butter has been added, continue to whip the buttercream until it's thick and smooth, 3 to 5 minutes. Again, this may take longer. Often when adding the butter, the mixture appears to deflate and even become soupy. Do not lose hope! Keep whipping! Beat in the vanilla toward the end.

recipe continues

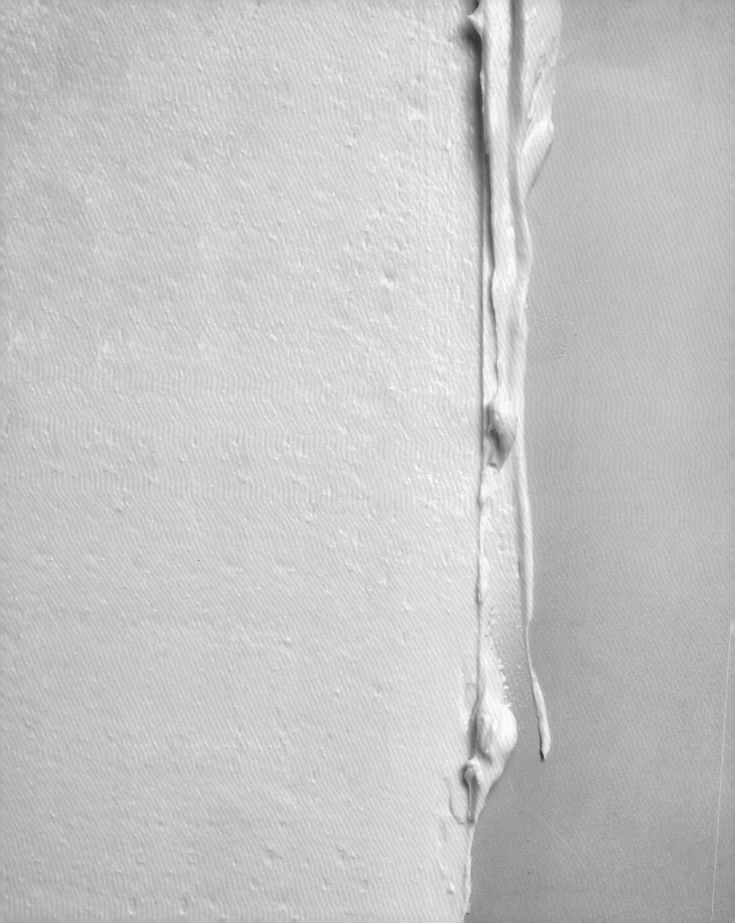

COFFEE BUTTERCREAM

½ cup instant coffee

2 tablespoons boiling water

TOOLS

Jar with a lid

1 Place the instant coffee into the jar. Pour the boiling water on top. Close the jar and shake until you can see the granules dissolving. Open the jar and allow the instant coffee concentrate to cool completely. (Save the extra concentrate to darken your buttercream.)

2 Add the instant coffee concentrate to the Vanilla buttercream as a final step, a little at a time, until you achieve the desired taste and color.

COOKIE BUTTER BUTTERCREAM

1 cup cookie butter

Add the cookie butter as the final step in the Vanilla buttercream recipe.

MINT BUTTERCREAM

⅛ teaspoon food-grade peppermint oil

6 drops green gel food coloring

6 drops teal gel food coloring

Add the peppermint oil as the final step in the Vanilla buttercream recipe. Add the food coloring little by little, starting with 2 drops of each color, until you have achieved the desired shade.

CARAMEL OR MAPLE BUTTERCREAM

1 cup caramel, or maple caramel completely cooled

Add the caramel as the final step in the Vanilla buttercream recipe.

CHOCOLATE COOKIE CRUMB BUTTERCREAM

½ cup chocolate cookie crumbs

Add the chocolate cookie crumbs as the final step in the Vanilla buttercream recipe.

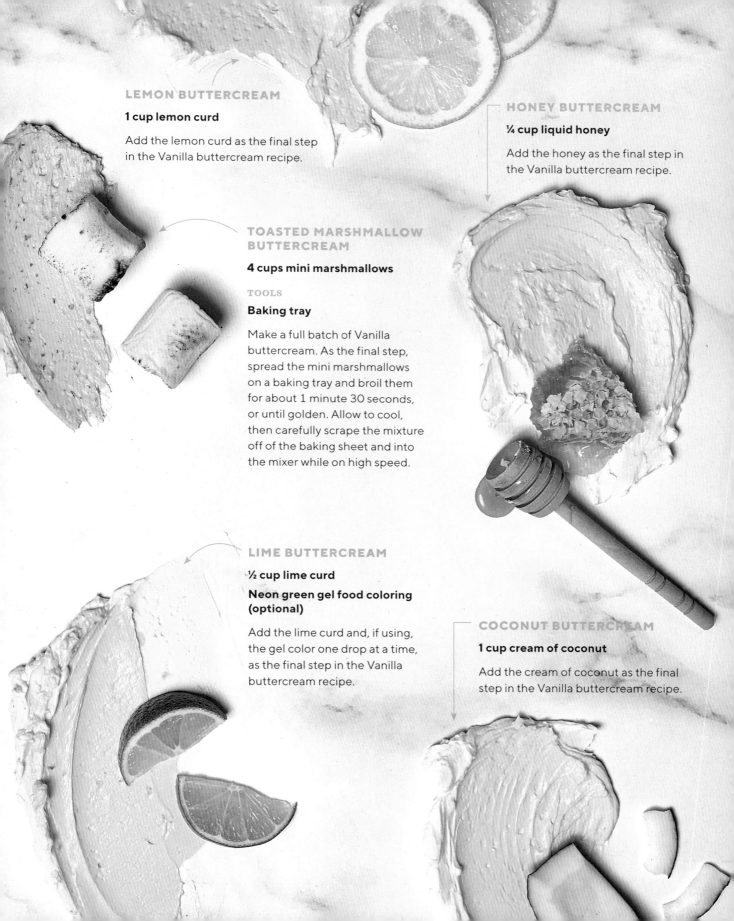

LEMON BUTTERCREAM

1 cup lemon curd

Add the lemon curd as the final step in the Vanilla buttercream recipe.

HONEY BUTTERCREAM

¼ cup liquid honey

Add the honey as the final step in the Vanilla buttercream recipe.

TOASTED MARSHMALLOW BUTTERCREAM

4 cups mini marshmallows

TOOLS

Baking tray

Make a full batch of Vanilla buttercream. As the final step, spread the mini marshmallows on a baking tray and broil them for about 1 minute 30 seconds, or until golden. Allow to cool, then carefully scrape the mixture off of the baking sheet and into the mixer while on high speed.

LIME BUTTERCREAM

½ cup lime curd
Neon green gel food coloring (optional)

Add the lime curd and, if using, the gel color one drop at a time, as the final step in the Vanilla buttercream recipe.

COCONUT BUTTERCREAM

1 cup cream of coconut

Add the cream of coconut as the final step in the Vanilla buttercream recipe.

rich Buttercream

This Italian meringue buttercream uses whole eggs instead of egg whites, which results in the richest buttercream of all. The yolks provide a natural creamy color and a luscious velvety texture.

• MAKES 4½ CUPS •

1¾ cups granulated sugar

½ cup water

5 large eggs, room temperature

2½ cups (5 sticks) unsalted butter, cut into tablespoon-size pieces, room temperature

1 teaspoon pure vanilla extract

TOOLS

Medium saucepan

Candy thermometer

Stand mixer with whisk attachment

Rubber spatula

1 In a small saucepan, combine the sugar and water. Place over medium heat and bring to a boil. Clip a candy thermometer to the side of the saucepan.

2 While the sugar syrup is heating, put the eggs in the bowl of a stand mixer fitted with the whisk attachment.

3 When the syrup reaches 230°F on the candy thermometer, begin to whip the eggs on medium-high speed. Whip until the eggs are frothy and light in color. The idea is to get the eggs frothy and light by the time your syrup reaches 240°F so that you can then move to the next step.

4 When the syrup reaches 240°F, immediately remove the pan from the heat and, with the mixer running, pour the syrup into the eggs in a very thin stream. Pour the syrup between the side of the bowl and the whisk attachment. Be very careful; this syrup is HOT! You do not want it to hit the whisk attachment and splash you.

5 Whip the eggs and sugar at high speed until thick and glossy and the bowl is no longer warm on the outside, about 8 to 12 minutes. The most important thing is to let the mixture cool down completely. When you touch the side of the bowl, you shouldn't feel any heat. This may take longer for you, or it may happen faster.

6 With the mixer running, add the butter, a piece at a time until all you have added all the butter. Scrape down the sides of the bowl with a spatula occasionally.

7 After all the butter has been added, add in the vanilla and continue to whip the buttercream until it's thick and smooth, 3 to 5 minutes. Again, this may take longer! Often, when adding the butter the mixture appears to deflate and even become soupy. Do not lose hope! Keep whipping!

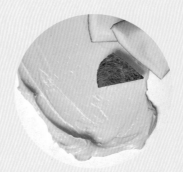

COCONUT RICH BUTTERCREAM

1 cup cream of coconut

Add the cream of coconut as the final step in the rich buttercream recipe.

Brown Sugar Buttercream

In this Swiss meringue buttercream I swapped out
white sugar for brown, giving it a more molasses-infused flavor.
It is rich and creamy with a hint of caramel tones from the
brown sugar, and pairs well with any cake recipe.

• MAKES 4½ CUPS •

**6 large egg whites, room
temperature**

**1 ¾ cups dark brown sugar,
packed**

½ teaspoon salt

**2½ cups (5 sticks) unsalted butter
cut into tablespoon-size pieces,
room temperature**

½ teaspoon pure vanilla extract

TOOLS

**Stand mixer with whisk
attachment**

Medium saucepan

Candy thermometer

Whisk

Rubber spatula

1 In the bowl of a stand mixer
fitted with the whisk attachment,
whisk the egg whites, brown sugar,
and salt.

2 Place the bowl over a saucepan
of simmering water. Continue to
whisk and heat until the mixture
reaches 160°F on a candy
thermometer.

3 Place the bowl back onto
the stand mixer with the whisk
attachment, then whisk until the
mixture is cool and fluffy. The bowl
should be cool/room temperature
to the touch.

4 With the mixer running, add the
butter, a piece at a time until all you
have added all the butter. Scrape
down the sides of the bowl with a
spatula occasionally.

5 Add the vanilla and mix until
blended.

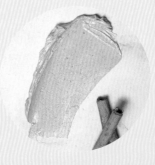

CINNAMON BROWN SUGAR BUTTERCREAM

1 tablespoon ground cinnamon

Add the cinnamon as the final step
in the brown sugar buttercream.

MAPLE BROWN SUGAR BUTTERCREAM

½ cup pure maple syrup

Add the maple syrup as the final step
in the brown sugar buttercream.

chocolate buttercream

I love this Swiss meringue buttercream because it is light and smooth as well as delightfully chocolaty. It isn't too rich, so it pairs perfectly with any cake, satisfying chocolate cravings without overpowering other flavors.

• MAKES 5 CUPS •

18 ounces good-quality dark chocolate (I use between 56% and 72%)

1 cup granulated sugar

¼ teaspoon salt

⅛ teaspoon cream of tartar

4 large egg whites, room temperature

2 cups (4 sticks) unsalted butter, cut into tablespoon-size pieces, room temperature

TOOLS

Heatproof bowl

Medium saucepan

Rubber spatula

Stand mixer with whisk attachment

Whisk

Kitchen scale

Chef's knife

Cutting board

1 Chop the chocolate as finely as you can and place into the heatproof bowl. Set the bowl over a saucepan of lightly simmering water (do not let the bowl touch the water). Melt the chocolate, stirring until smooth, then set the bowl aside to cool while you prepare the buttercream. Leave the saucepan of water on the stove, as you will need it shortly.

2 In the bowl of a stand mixer fitted with the whisk attachment, whisk the sugar, salt, and cream of tartar. Whisk in the egg whites until thoroughly combined.

3 Place the bowl with the egg whites over the saucepan of simmering water (again, do not let the bowl touch the water). Heat the mixture, whisking frequently, and the sugar is mostly dissolved. It should be warm but not hot to the touch, about 2 to 5 minutes. You should feel just a little grittiness when you rub a bit of the mixture between your fingertips.

4 Transfer the bowl to the stand mixer and fit the mixer with the whisk attachment. Whip at high speed until thick and glossy and the bowl is no longer warm on the outside, about 5 minutes.

5 With the mixer running, add the butter, a piece at a time until all you have added all the butter. Scrape down the sides of the bowl with a spatula occasionally.

6 After all the butter has been added, continue to whip the buttercream until it is thick and smooth, about 3 to 5 minutes.

7 Check the melted chocolate: it should be soft and liquid, not firm; if it's completely cooled and thickened, set the bowl over the still-hot water in the saucepan for just a few seconds and stir until it is soft but not warm. Scrape the chocolate into the buttercream and whip on high speed until fully incorporated.

CHOCOLATE HAZELNUT BUTTERCREAM

8 ounces chocolate hazelnut spread

Omit 8 ounces of the quality dark chocolate, and replace with 8 ounces of chocolate hazelnut spread. Add as the final step to your buttercream.

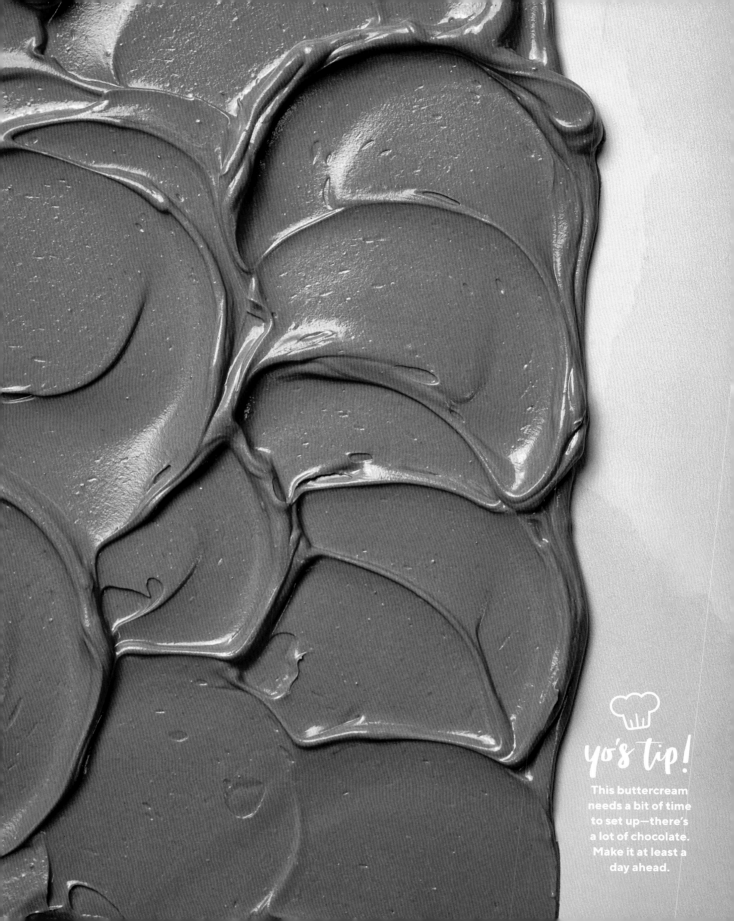

yo's tip!

This buttercream
needs a bit of time
to set up—there's
a lot of chocolate.
Make it at least a
day ahead.

dark chocolate ganache

Ganache is one of my favorite ways to incorporate chocolate into a cake. It's simple, rich, and about as close to pure melted chocolate as you can get. This proportion of chocolate to cream (1:1 by weight) makes a pourable ganache that firms up to a creamy, smooth spreadable consistency when cool.

• MAKES 4 CUPS •

1 pound good-quality dark chocolate (between 56% and 72%)

2 cups heavy whipping cream (35%)

TOOLS

Kitchen scale

Chef's knife

Cutting board

Medium heatproof bowl

Medium heavy bottomed saucepan

Lid or large plate

Rubber spatula

Sieve

Medium bowl

1 Chop the chocolate as finely as you can. Place it in a heatproof bowl.

2 Pour the cream into a heavy saucepan and place over medium-high heat. Bring just to a simmer. You should see bubbles around the edges of the saucepan and movement just under the surface of the cream. Do not let it boil.

3 Pour the hot cream over the chocolate and cover the bowl with a lid. Let stand for 10 to 15 minutes.

4 Uncover the bowl and gently stir with a spatula, starting in the middle and working your way out. The ganache will start to darken and come together into a velvety mixture. To ensure that no lumps are left, pour the ganache through a sieve into a clean bowl.

5 Use the ganache right away for drizzling or creating a drip. Or cover and let it cool for several hours or overnight at room temperature if you're spreading it as icing.

BLACK CHOCOLATE GANACHE

1 tablespoon black gel food coloring

Add the black gel food coloring to the chocolate and cream in step 4 before stirring.

yo's tip!

If the ganache becomes too firm to spread as you're working with it, gently reheat it in the microwave for 10 seconds at a time, stirring frequently, until spreadable.

cream cheese frosting

This frosting is smooth and creamy with a balance of sweet and tangy flavor provided by the cream cheese. It is easy to spread and pairs well in any cake.

• MAKES 3 CUPS •

1 cup (1 block) cream cheese, room temperature

1 teaspoon pure vanilla extract

½ cup (1 stick) unsalted butter, room temperature

4 cups of icing sugar, sifted

TOOLS

Sieve

Stand mixer with paddle attachment

Rubber spatula

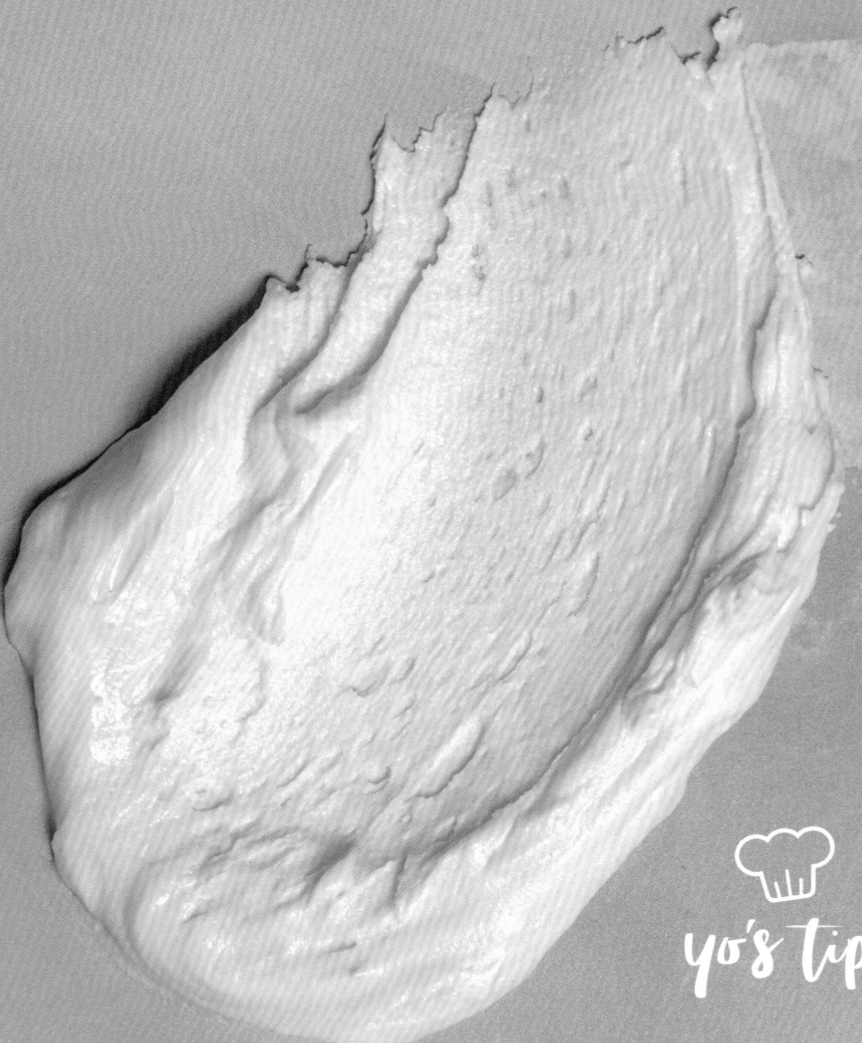

1 Beat cream cheese and vanilla in the bowl of a stand mixer fitted with a paddle attachment until smooth for about 3 minutes. Make sure to beat the cream cheese well before adding butter to avoid any lumps.

2 Slowly add in the butter and beat for another 2 minutes. Once smooth, make sure to scrape down the sides and bottom of the bowl with a rubber spatula.

3 At low speed, add icing sugar and mix until fully incorporated. Beat for 2 minutes at high speed to remove any lumps.

yo's tip!

To adjust the consistency of your frosting if it feels too soft, simply sift in more icing sugar to stiffen.

peanut butter frosting

If you're a fan of peanut butter, then you'll go NUTS for my easy peanut butter frosting recipe. It tastes similar to the filling in a peanut butter cup, with a spreadable consistency.

• **MAKES 1½ CUPS** •

½ cup + 2 tablespoons smooth peanut butter

¼ cup (½ stick) unsalted butter, room temperature

¾ cup icing sugar, sifted

2 tablespoons heavy whipping cream (35%)

TOOLS

Sieve

Stand mixer with paddle attachment

1 In the bowl of a stand mixer fitted with the paddle attachment, cream the peanut butter and butter together on low speed until well blended.

2 Add the icing sugar and beat until incorporated. Turn the mixer up to medium-high speed to beat out any lumps.

3 Turn the mixer to low and pour in the cream.

4 Once again, turn the mixer to medium-high speed and beat frosting for 1 minute, until smooth and fully mixed.

caramel

I love caramel. The rich, buttery flavor and the ooey-gooey consistency. It makes everything better.

• MAKES 1 CUP •

1 cup + 2 tablespoons granulated sugar

3 tablespoons water

¼ cup (½ stick) unsalted butter, cold

½ cup heavy whipping cream (35%)

TOOLS

Medium saucepan

Medium heatproof bowl

Sieve

Small microwave-safe bowl

Wooden spoon

1 Place the sugar and water in the saucepan and heat over medium-low.

2 Meanwhile, place the butter into the heatproof bowl and rest a sieve on top.

3 Heat the heavy cream in the microwave for about 1 minute, or until hot.

4 Watch the sugar until it starts changing color. Once amber in color, use a wooden spoon to stir the sugar until even in color. Remove the saucepan from the heat.

5 Slowly pour half of the hot heavy cream into the sugar mixture, stirring carefully. Pour in the remaining hot cream and stir until combined.

6 Pour the sugar and cream mixture through the sieve onto the cold butter. Let the butter melt into the mixture for about 5 minutes.

7 Gently stir the mixture until it comes together.

8 Set aside to cool completely and thicken.

MAPLE CARAMEL

3 tablespoons pure maple syrup

Place maple syrup in the bowl with the butter in step 2 of the recipe.

yo's tip!

You only need one batch of caramel to flavor the caramel buttercream. The remaining will fill the Caramel Cone Cake (page 90).

hump day

People always ask me, "What do you do with your cake humps?" I often turn them into mini cakes or my version of mug cakes. I use circle cutters to create little layers out of my humps, and then I have fun filling and stacking them with leftover simple syrup, buttercream, ganache, frosting—whatever I feel like. These are sweet little treats you can give to friends, take to work, or surprise your kids with the best afternoon snack when they arrive home from school.

mix & match

Here are a few suggestions for flavor combinations for those days when you don't have time to layer all the way up. We all have those days...

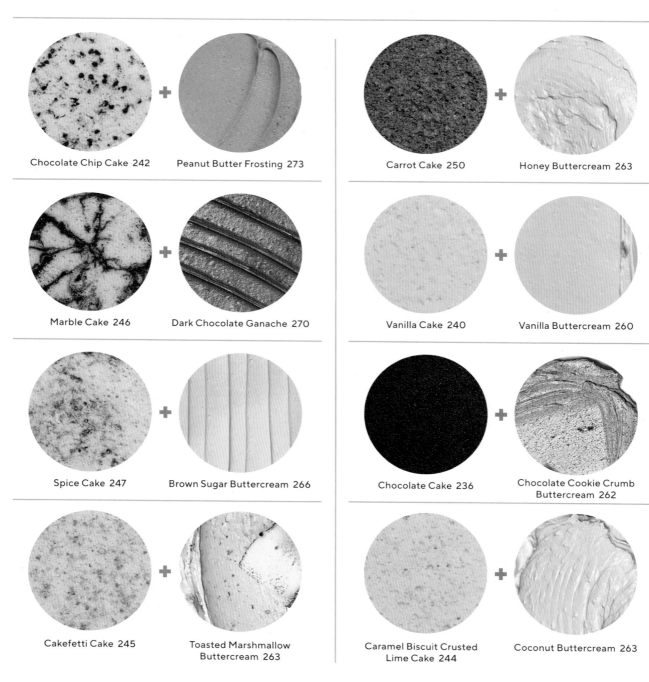

Chocolate Chip Cake 242 + Peanut Butter Frosting 273

Carrot Cake 250 + Honey Buttercream 263

Marble Cake 246 + Dark Chocolate Ganache 270

Vanilla Cake 240 + Vanilla Buttercream 260

Spice Cake 247 + Brown Sugar Buttercream 266

Chocolate Cake 236 + Chocolate Cookie Crumb Buttercream 262

Cakefetti Cake 245 + Toasted Marshmallow Buttercream 263

Caramel Biscuit Crusted Lime Cake 244 + Coconut Buttercream 263

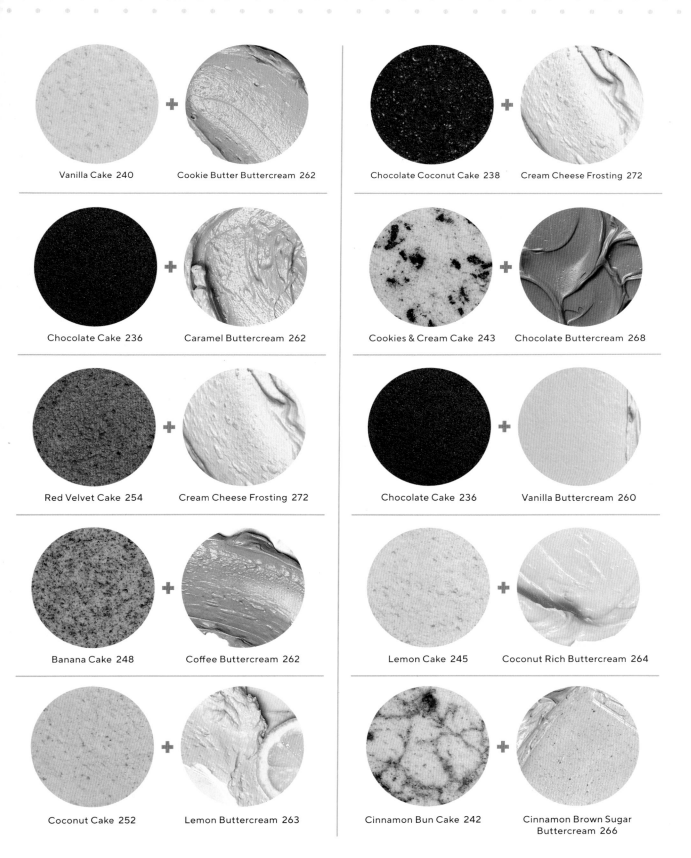

Vanilla Cake 240 + Cookie Butter Buttercream 262

Chocolate Coconut Cake 238 + Cream Cheese Frosting 272

Chocolate Cake 236 + Caramel Buttercream 262

Cookies & Cream Cake 243 + Chocolate Buttercream 268

Red Velvet Cake 254 + Cream Cheese Frosting 272

Chocolate Cake 236 + Vanilla Buttercream 260

Banana Cake 248 + Coffee Buttercream 262

Lemon Cake 245 + Coconut Rich Buttercream 264

Coconut Cake 252 + Lemon Buttercream 263

Cinnamon Bun Cake 242 + Cinnamon Brown Sugar Buttercream 266

let them eat cake!

HOW TO Cut it

Cakes can be a challenge to cut. My best advice is to use a sharp chef's knife or serrated knife. Have a jug of hot water and two clean cloths at your side, one wet and one dry. Dip the blade of the knife into the hot water, and wipe the water off the blade with the dry cloth. Use the damp cloth to wipe crumbs and buttercream off the knife after each cut and before dipping the knife into hot water again.

HOW TO Admire it

Just look at this masterpiece you created! Of course cakes look beautiful and tempting once they are complete and decorated—but why does it have to end there? Cake is meant to be cut, shared, and devoured! Take the time to present your slices on gorgeous plates with a little garnish if you feel like taking that extra step. Your guests will be delighted at the sight of the decadent layers and textures that you masterfully crafted. They will be even more delighted once they take that first bite.

HOW TO Keep it

If you are not cutting the entire cake in one sitting, make sure to protect and store the leftovers. You can enjoy more slices of cake for days to come! Cover the exposed interior surface of the remaining cake with plastic wrap pressed tightly against the surface. If the remaining cake is too small to continue standing, carefully lay it down, and make sure to wrap the exposed bottom layer as well.

HOW TO Enjoy it

I can't stress this enough—cake should be eaten at room temperature. Your refrigerator is your best friend while you are building and decorating a cake, but now it's time for you and your friend to part ways. Buttercream, ganache, and frostings all firm up in the fridge, and they need time to return back into their natural creamy consistency. The cake layers themselves warm up for a more relaxed texture. You want the flavors to hit your palate as soon as you take the first bite without any resistance from the cold.

how to store it

CAKE LAYERS

I prefer to leave cooled cakes in the pan and place plastic wrap directly on the surface of the cake. Then wrap the entire cake pan in plastic wrap. Freezing cakes in their pans maintains the shape perfectly and allows you to stack them to save room in your freezer. If you need your cake pans for another project, you can carefully remove the cakes from the pans and wrap each one with two layers of plastic wrap. Place the cakes in a safe spot in the freezer, making sure not to rest anything on top until they are frozen solid.

TO THAW, place them in the fridge and allow them to thaw overnight, while still in their pans or wrapped in plastic.

SIMPLE SYRUP

Pour the cooled syrup into an airtight container and store in the fridge for up to one month. Alternatively, you can freeze the syrup for up to three months. If you are unsure of what to do with leftover simple syrups, you can also make cocktails, sodas, or lemonade by simply pouring a little syrup into a glass over ice and diluting it with flat or sparkling water or club soda.

TO THAW, place the container of syrup in the fridge and allow it to thaw overnight.

BUTTERCREAM

Store buttercream in a cool dry place for up to one day. If you are making it more than a day in advance, transfer to an airtight container and store in the fridge for up to one week or the freezer for up to one month.

TO THAW, remove the container of buttercream from the fridge or freezer and allow to sit out overnight at room temperature.

GANACHE

I recommend using ganache as soon as it has reached the desired spreadable consistency. If you have leftover ganache, transfer to an airtight container and store in the fridge for up to one week, or in the freezer for up to two months. Leftover ganache is delightful when spread between two cookies to make a sandwich, or gently heated and poured over ice cream.

TO THAW, remove the container of ganache from the fridge or freezer and allow to sit out overnight at room temperature. You may need to gently defrost the ganache in the microwave in ten-second increments in order to bring it back to the desired consistency. Over-stirring ganache will cause splitting.

CARAMEL

Store caramel in an airtight container or a squeeze bottle with a cap in the fridge for up to one month, or in the freezer for up to three months. Extra caramel is delicious on toast with peanut butter, drizzled over a bowl of ice cream, or squeezed onto a piece of chocolate.

TO THAW, remove the container from the freezer and place it in the fridge to thaw overnight.

FROSTING

Frosting is best when freshly made, and it is so simple and quick that there is no need to make ahead. If you have leftover frosting, store it in an airtight container with plastic wrap directly on the surface and a lid on top. Frosting crusts over when exposed to air. Store the frosting in the fridge for a few days, or in the freezer for up to one month. Use leftover frosting to make mini cakes and mug cakes out of cake humps. (page 000)

TO THAW, allow the container of frosting to sit out at room temperature to thaw overnight. Stir until smooth.

xo,
Yo

want more?

Your caking journey
doesn't have to
end here!

At How To Cake It, we teach, inspire, and transform you into a better baker. How? With courses, live classes, premium products, and our incredible collective of world-class sweet artists, like Yolanda, to guide you every step of the way.

Join our global community of millions of baking and sweets enthusiasts.

www.howtocakeit.com

Twitter: @yolanda_gampp
Instagram: @yolanda_gampp
Tik Tok: @how.to.cake.it
Pinterest: How To Cake It
Facebook: How To Cake It

SCAN HERE
to become a better baker.

thank you

A big and warm thank-you to our licensing guru and dear friend **STEVEN HELLER** for connecting us with the amazing **KAREN KILPATRICK** of Kayppin Media. Karen, without you, How To Cake It Books would not have been born. Thank you for creating such a supportive (and needed) new publishing model that empowers creatives—and thank you for all your enthusiasm, help, and dedication throughout this whole process. We could not have asked for a better partner to help make this dream come true.

CONNIE CONTARDI Connie, or shall I call you the dreamweaver? Thank you for hearing me, seeing me, and always being my friend. I am in awe of your positivity, strength, and childlike wonder. You always dream big and encourage others to do the same. I tell you I want to write another book and you respond with, "Let's launch How To Cake It Books and be publishers!" Mind. Blown. I wouldn't expect anything less.

JOCELYN MERCER Just look at how we have leveled up! No one told us building a business would be easy, but no one thought we'd have this much fun. I consider myself lucky to be on this journey with you as we grow our company. When I think about the growth our team and company have made over the years it truly amazes me. Where to next?

EUGENIA ZYKOVA Eugenia, you're a Eugenius! See what I did there? Working with you has been an absolute delight and a dream come true. You are beyond good at what you do and you made my creations come to life. I appreciate your patience, professionalism, and collaboration—my pepper mill collection enjoyed working with you immensely. From the first day on set, I knew we had made the right decision and felt relaxed knowing that my cakes and I were in good hands. Thank you so much for all your hard work.

LAURA PALESE You are a delight. Warm, helpful, and encouraging from the start. Your portfolio truly speaks for itself, and your talent is obvious—a true powerhouse. When I first saw the design you created for this book I had to pick my jaw up off the floor. I don't think I have really recovered. Thank you for helping to make my vision a reality in such a beautiful way.

HELENA YUU Having you by my side for this process has been incredible. Your willingness to learn, your hard work and hours on your feet, and most important, your honest opinion. I really appreciate it and thank you from the bottom of my heart. Sometimes you need someone to tell you you've gone overboard with the honey in your buttercream. Because of you, I know we will always have cones in different area codes and plastic on our peelers. Thanks, PC.

KAM GREWAL I think at this point you can have business cards printed with the title "Production Publishing Manager." You did an excellent job and were a tremendous help to me and the team. Thank you for listening to all my random cake thoughts and exclamations and organizing them into reminders and documents while I worked in the kitchen. Your '90s R&B playlists provided the perfect backdrop. The teenage girl in me is still singing.

HTCI TEAM Thank you to the entire HTCI team. Look at us go! They say it takes a village and in our case Connie, Jocelyn, and I have built one that we are really proud of. Thank you all for your hard work and desire to grow along with us. The three of us had big dreams for this journey and you have all played a role in that.

ORHAN SUMEN Oh, Orhan, what would I do without you? You have been instrumental in the growth of How To Cake It as a whole. You walk me through all my breakdowns, understand my sarcasm perfectly, and calmly guide me where I need to go and remind me of everything I need to do. I don't think I can ever allow you to become the big-time screenwriting director you want to be—we need you, Slateman!

CENGIZ ERCAN I've told you this many times, and I am writing it here as proof: when you become a famous nature photographer and you are camped out in the mountains of Nepal waiting for a snow leopard to appear, you are going to miss all these bowls of buttercream. Mark my words! Thank you for your years of hard work and dedication to How To Cake It, and for putting up with me and my "jokes".

JARED MACPHERSON Thank you to Jared, How To Cake It's talented Head of Design, for all the ways you elevate our brand aesthetically. We are so grateful for you squeezing in all our urgent and last-minute requests on top of ALL the other endless design tasks you do for us, too! We appreciate you so much and owe this book cover design—and our How To Cake It Books imprint logo—to you!

SHANNON MURPHY Shannon, thank you for the care you put into recipe testing and your helpful notes and input. As usual, you were a tremendous help to me and I am so grateful! The minute I started to write this book I said, "I think Shannon would be a great recipe tester." I was right, and you exceeded my expectations. You also went above and beyond in assisting us with your proofreading skills. I hope you're ready for my next book! I'm not ready yet, so you have a bit of time to prepare . . .

PAMELA SMITH Have you seen what I look like in this book! You did that, Pamela!! Thank you for making me look and feel beautiful. You are a pleasure to have on set and you go above and beyond—making giant fondant sprinkles, steaming my dress, and helping out the whole team. Thank you for your hard work and being a team player. I can't wait for another chance to look glam again.

HAYLEY JOZWIAK Thank you for your copy editing skills. You did a great job of editing my thoughts on paper and making them coherent. Copy editing was a vital part of the process—it helped communicate my stories and recipes to my amazing baking community. They put up with my casual cake talk on YouTube but I needed this book to level up. Now I'm worried that you'll have to edit this thank-you . . .

HOW TO CAKE IT COMMUNITY Thank you for all your support and for being the most enthusiastic, encouraging set of bakers on the planet ! We couldn't do this without you.

ANN MARIE Thank you for helping me grow and to see my self more clearly. Your guidance has been truly invaluable to me.

SUAD, BIANCA, CASPAR & DEREK In order of how we met. Thank you to my BFFs for always being there to listen . . . and to smack sense into me. ♥ you all!

D&P I saved the best for last. Thanks to my two favorite guys! The loves of my life . . . and my built-in managers. You always support me and display your pride and confidence in me. With that, I know I can do anything. The best part is coming home to the two of you. Thank you for always believing in me as much as I believe in you.

index

ABOUT THE AUTHOR With over 4.5 million YouTube subscribers and 2.8 million Instagram followers, the star of How To Cake It, Yolanda, is a self-taught cake artist with over twenty years of experience. And has been featured on the *Today* show, *Good Morning America*, *The Kelly Clarkson Show*, *Live with Kelly and Ryan*, Netflix's *Nailed It*, *Best Baker in America*, *Cake Wars* and *Crime Scene Kitchen* to name a few.

While turning cake into pretty much anything, Yolanda, a bestselling author affectionately nicknamed by her fans as the 'Beyoncé of Cakes', entertains with her irresistible personality, laughs at her own mistakes, and is one of the most respected and celebrated celebrity cake artists in the world.